Prince William County, Virginia

District Court Orders

1793 (Part 2)

Ruth and Sam Sparacio

Heritage Books
2025

HERITAGE BOOKS

AN IMPRINT OF HERITAGE BOOKS, INC.

Books, CDs, and more—Worldwide

For our listing of thousands of titles see our website
at
www.HeritageBooks.com

Published 2025 by
HERITAGE BOOKS, INC.
Publishing Division
5810 Ruatan Street
Berwyn Heights, MD 20740

International Standard Book Number
Paperbound: 978-1-68034-451-6

PRINCE WILLIAM COUNTY, VIRGINIA DISTRICT COURT ORDER BOOK 1793

DUMFRIES DISTRICT COURT, OCTOBER 1793

p.
169
<u>Alexander & Muschett v Stith & Boggess</u>

The Commonwealth of Virginia to the Sheriff of FAIRFAX County, Greeting;
We command you that you take BUCKNER STITH and ROBERT BOGGESS
if they be found within your Bailiwick and them safely keep so that you have their
bodies before the Judges of the District Court to be held at the Town of DUMFRIES
at the next Court to answer WILLIAM ALEXANDER and JAMES MUSCHETT of a
Plea of Debt for two hundred pounds current money of Virginia, damage five pounds,
And have then there this Writ. Witness GEORGE BROOKE, Clerk of the Court at
DUMFRIES the first day of April in the 14th year of the Commonwealth A.D. 1790
G. BROOKE, C. D. D. C.

For Debt due on Bond and Bail required
Executed.   CHARLES TURNER, D. S.

FAIRFAX County to wit;
WILLIAM ALEXANDER and JAMES MUSCHETT complain of BUCKNER
STITH and ROBERT BOGGESS, both in the custody of the Sheriff of the County of a
Plea that they render to them the sum of two hundred pounds current money of Virginia which to them, WILLIAM and JAMES, the Defendants owe and from WILLIAM
and JAMES unjustly detain for that, to wit, that whereas the Defendants by their
certain Writing Obligatory sealed with their seals and dated the sixteenth day of December in the year of our Lord 1789, acknowlowledged themselves to be bound to the
Plaintiffs in the sum of two hundred pounds current money of Virginia and for the
payment thereof to the Plaintiffs their certain Attorney Executors Administrators or
assigns, Nevertheless the Defendants though often required by the Plaintiffs have not
nor has either of them paid the Plaintiffs or either of the Plaintiffs the sum of two
hundred pounds as aforesaid or any part thereof wherefore the Plaintiffs say they are
injured and have damage to the value of [blank]

p.
170
<u>Alexander & Muschett v Stith & Boggess</u>

and thereupon they bring suit and they bring here into Court the Writing
Obligatory which testifies the Debt in form aforesaid
RICHARD BRENT for Plaintiffs

Pledges of	]	John Doe &
Prosecution	]	Richd. Roe
June 1790		Bail & Common Order against Defendants
July 1790		Common Order confirmed
October 1790		Common Order set aside and payment joined

KNOW ALL MEN by these presents that we BUCKNER STITH and
ROBERT BOGGESS of FAIRFAX County and State of Virginia are held and firmly

bound unto WILLIAM ALEXANDER and JAMES MUSCHETT of Prince William County and State aforesaid in the full and just sum of two hundred pounds current money of Virginia to be paid unto WILLIAM ALEXANDER and JAMES MUS-CHETT their certain Attorney Executors Administrators or assigns to the which payment well and truly to be made and done we bind ourselves and each of our heirs jointly and severally our Executors Administrators and assigns firmly by these presents, Sealed with our seals and dated the sixteenth day of December in the year of our Lord one thousand seven hundred and eighty nine

 THE CONDITION of the above obligation is such that if the above bound BUCK-NER STITH and ROBERT BOGGESS do and shall well and truly pay or cause to be paid unto WILLIAM ALEXANDER and JAMES MUSCHETT their certain Attorney Executors Administrators of assigns the full and just sum of two hundred pounds of the aforesaid money at or upon the first day of March next ensuing, then the above Obligation to be void or else to remain in full force and virtue in Law
Sealed and delivered in the presence of
   JOS: KIRBY   BUCKNER STITH
                   ROBERT BOGGESS

p.   <u>Alexander & Muscett v Stith & Boggess</u>
171   Memorandum: That upon the 17th day of May 1790 personally appeared
    before me, THOMAS POLLARD, one of the Justices of the Peace for FAIR-FAX, JOHN HAWKINS of the County and undertook for BUCKNER STITH at the suit of MUSCHETT & ALEXANDER in an action of Debt depending in the District Court that if BUCKNER STITH shall be cast in the suit that he, BUCKNER STITH, shall satisfy and pay the condemnation of the Court or that he, JOHN HAWKINS, will do it for him; Acknowledged before me
             THOS: POLLARD

October 15, 1793
    WILLIAM ALEXANDER & JAMES MUSCHETT, Plaintiffs   ]
       against   ]   In Debt
    BUCKNER STITH & ROBERT BOGGESS, Defendants   ]
 This day came the parties by their Attornies and this suit abates as to the Defendant, BUCKNER STITH, by his death and the Defendant, ROBERT BOGGESS, relinquishing his former Plea acknowledged the action of the Plaintiffs against him; therefore it is considered by the Court that the Plaintiffs recover against the Defendant two hundred pounds current money of Virginia, the Debt in the Declaration mentioned, and their costs by them about their suit in this behalf expended, and the Defendant in mercy, &c. But this Judgment may be discharged by the payment of one hundred pounds of the aforesaid money with Interest thereon to be computed after the rate of five per cent per annum from the first day of March seventeen hundred and ninety untill paid and the costs
    Plaintiffs's costs   190 lbs tobacco @ 1 1/2   ]
            60 lbs tobacco @ 1 1/4   ] p pound & $8.36.
    Execution issued

p.   Stuart & Muschett v Jackson
172   The Commonwealth of Virginia to the Sheriff of Prince William County
Greeting. We command you that you take FRANCIS SON otherwise called
FRANCIS JACKSON in custody & so forth of a Plea that he, the Defendant, render
to them, HUGH & JAMES, the Plaintiffs, the sum of thirty eight pounds, fifteen
shillings and ten pence wich to them the Defendant owes and from them unjustly
detains for that, to wit, that whereas the Defendant on the first day of January in the
year of our Lord one thousand seven hundred and eighty seven at the Parish of
Dettingen and County of Prince William by his certain Bill Obligatory sealed with the
seal of the Defendant and dated on the day and year aforesaid, and to the Court now
here shewn promised to pay HUGH STUART and JAMES MUSCHETT or order on
demand the sum of nineteen pounds, seven shillings and eleven pence for value received, and for the same payment well and truly to be made the Defendant by the
same Bill firmly bound himself his heirs Executors and Administrators in the penal
sum of thirty eight pounds, fifteen shillings and ten pence; And the Plaintiffs saith and
avereth that in fact the Defendant did not pay the sum of nineteen pounds, seven
shillings and eleven pence unto the Plaintiffs or their Attorney or order which

p.   Stuart & Muschett v Jackosn
173   he ought to have paid to the Plaintiffs according to the form and effect of the
Bill whereby an action hath accrued to the Plaintiffs to demand and have of the
Defendant the penal sum of thirty eight pounds, fifteen shillings and ten pence, yet
the Defendant though often required by the Plaintiffs hath not paid the thirty eight
pounds, fifteen shillings and ten pence to the Plaintiffs but hath hitherto and still does
refuse to pay the same to the Plaintiffs to the damage of the Plaintiffs five pounds
and therefore they produce the suit and so forth

                         EDMUND RANDOLPH for Plaintiffs

Pledges of prosecution   `]
John Doe & Richard Roe]
    June 1790   Common Order against Defendant and Sheriff
    July 1790   Common Order confirmed
    October 1790   Common Order set aside and payment joined

    Memorandum that on the sixth day of May 1790 personally appeared before
me, ALEXANDER BROWN, a Justice of the Peace for the County of Prince William,
SAMUEL JACKSON and undertook for FRANCIS JACKSON at the suit of HUGH
STEWART and JAMES MUSCHETT that if FRANCIS JACKSON should be cast
that he should pay the costs and condemnation of the Court or render his body to Prison in saatisfaction for the same or that he, SAMUEL JACKSON, would do it for
him. Given under my hand the date above

                         ALEXR: BROWN

    I promise to pay to HUGH STEWART and JAMES MUSCHETT or order on
demand the just sum of nineteen pounds, seven shillings and eleven pence for value
received, to which payment I bind myself my heirs Executors and Administrators in
the penal sum of thirty eight pounds, fifteen shillings and ten pence as witness my
hand and seal this first day of January in the year one thousand seven hundred and
eighty seven

Sealed and delivered in the presence of
  MUNGO M. HANCOCK   FRANCIS SON   [seal]
  1789 July 2d. Payment received   12/6.

p.   Stuart & Muschett v Jackson
174   October 15, 1793
        HUGH STUART & JAMES MUSCHETT, Plaintiffs   ]
            against   ] In Debt
        FRANCIS SON othwise called FRANCIS JACKSON, Defendant]
    This day came the parties by their Attornies and the Defendant relinquishing his
former Plea acknowledged the Plaintiffs's action against him; therefore it is considered by the Court that the Plaintiffs recover against the Defendant thirty eight
pounds, fifteen shillings and ten pence, the Debt in the Declaration mentioned and
their costs by them about their suit in this behalf expended and the Defendant in
mercy, &c. But this Judgment may be discharged by the payment of nineteen
pounds, seven shillings and eleven pence with Interest thereon to be computed after
the rate of five percentum per annum from the first day of January 1787 untill paid
and the costs. The Defendant is to have Credit for twelve shillings and six pence paid
the second day of July 1789
            Plaintiffs's costst   150 lbs tobacco @ 1 1/2   ]
                                    60 lbs tobacco @ 1 1/4   ] p pound. & $8.38
            Execution issued

        Cockran v Grant & Blackwell
        The Commonwealth of Virginia to the Sheriff of FAUQUIER County, Greeting.
We command you that you take WILLIAM GRANT and THOMAS BLACKWELL if
they be found within your Bailiwick and them safely keep so that you have their
bodies before the Judges of the District Court to be held at the Town of DUMFRIES
at the next Court to answer THOMAS COCKRAN, Assignee of WILLIAM THOMP-
SON, who was Assignee of JOHN THOMPSON, of a Plea of Debt for thirty six
pounds, thirteen shillngs current many of Virginia, damages ten pounds, and have
then there this Writ. Witness GEORGE BROOKE, Clerk of the Court at DUM-
FRIES the 14th day of April in the 14th year of the Commonwealth A.D. 1790
                            G. BROOKE C. D. D. C.
        For money due by single Bill, Bail is required
                            A. BUCHANNAN
        I will be Security for the within WILLIAM GRANT and THOMAS BLACK-
WELL agreeable to Law
                        WILLIAM BRENT
        Executed & Security Bond returned p
                        AUGUSTINE JENNINGS, D. S.

p.   Cockran v Grant & Blackwell
175   FAUQUIER County, to wit
        THOMAS COCKRAN who was Assignee of WILLIAM THOMPSON who was

Assignee of JOHN THOMPSON, complains of WILLIAM GRANT and THOMAS BLACKWELL in custody &c., of a Plea that they render unto the Plaintiff the sum of thirty six pounds, thirteen shillings current money of Virginia which they unjustly detain from him for this, to wit, that whereas the Defendants on the eighteenth day of August in the year of our Lord one thousand seven hundred and eighty nine at the County aforesaid by their certain Writing Obligatory sealed with their seals and to the Court now here shewn the date whereof is the same day and year acknowledged themselves to be held and firmly bound unto JOHN THOMPSON in the sum of thirty six pounds, thirteen shillings to be paid to JOHN THOMPSON on or before the first day of December then next and JOHN THOMPSON afterwards, to wit, on the twentieth day of February Anno Domini one thousand seven hundred and ninety at the County aforesaid by his certain indorsement on the Writing Obligatory did appoint and order the contents thereof to be paid to WILLIAM THOMPSON, who afterwards, to wit, on the same day and year at the County aforesaid, and before the money was paid by his indorsement thereon did appoint the same to be paid to the Plaintiff of which several Assignments the Defendants, afterwards, to wit, on the day and year last above mentioned had notice by virtue whereof and of the Act of Assembly in that case made and provided the Plaintiff became entitled to demand and have of the Defendants the sum of thirty six pounds, thirteen shillings, Nevertheless the Defendants although often requested have not yet paid the sum of thirty six pounds, thirteen shillings to the Plaintiff but hitherto to pay the same have refused and still do refuse to the damage of the Plaintiff of ten pounds, therefore he brings suit, &c.

A. BUCHANNAN for Plaintiff

Pledges &c. J. Doe & R. Roe

p.	Cockran v Grant & Blackwell	
176	June 1790	Common Order against Defendant & Security
	July 1790	Common Order confirmed
	October 1790	Special Bail, Common Order set aside and payment joined

KNOW ALL MEN by these presents that we WILLIAM GRANT, THOMAS BLACKWELL and WILLIAM BRENT are held and firmly bound unto THOMAS BRONAUGH, Gent., Sheriff, in the sum of seventy three pounds, six shillings to be paid to THOMAS BRONAUGH his certain Attorney his heirs Executors Administrators or assigns to which payment well and truly to be made we bind ourselves jointly and severally our joint and several heirs, Executors and Administrators firmly by these presents; Sealed with our seals and dated this eighth day of May 1790

THE CONDITION of the above obligation is such that if the above bound WILLIAM GRANT and THOMAS BLACKWELL shall make their personal appearance at the next District Court held in the Town of DUMFRIES then and there to answer the suit of THOMAS COCKRAN, Assignee of WILLIAM THOMPSON, who was Assignee of JOHN THOMPSON, in a Plea of Debt for thirty six pounds, thirteen shillings, damage ten pounds, then this Obligation to be void else to remain in full force and virtue

Sealed and delivered in presence of   W. GRANT [seal]

AUGUSTINE JENNINGS, D. C.   THO: BLACKWELL [seal]

THOS. BRENT; WILLIAM BRENT, JUNR. WM. BRENT   {seal

KNOW ALL MEN by these presents that we WILLIAM GRANT and THOMAS BLACKWELL of FAUQUIER County do promise to pay to JOHN THOMPSON his heirs Executors Administrators or assigns the sum of thirty six pounds, thirteen shillings current money of Virginia on or before the first day of December next for value received of him, to which payment well and truly to be made we bind outselves jointly and severallly our joint and several heirs Executors and Administrators firmly by these presents; Witness our hands and seals this 18th fay of August 1789

p.   Cockran v Grant & Blackwell
177   Sealed and delivered in presence of us
        BENJAMIN MAURY   WM. GRANT   [seal]
        JOHN GRANT   THO: BLACKWELL   [seal]

        I hereby assign my right and title to the within Bond to WILLIAM THOMP-
SON   JOHN THOMPSON
                                    February 20th 1790
        I do hereby assign all my right title and interest to the within Bond for value received to Mr. THOMAS COCKRANE

                                    WM. THOMPSON
October 15, 1793
        THOMAS COCKRAN, Assignee of WILLIAM THOMPSON,
        who was Assignee of JOHN THOMPSON, Plaintiffs   ]
                against   ] In Debt
        WILLIAM GRANT & THOMAS BLACKWELL, Defendants   ]
   This day came the parties by their Attornies and the Defendants relinquishing their former Plea acknowledged the Plaintiff's action against them; therefore it is considered by the Court that the Plaintiff recover against the Defendants thirty six pounds thirteen shillings current money of Virginia, the Debt in the Declaration mentioned and their costs by them about their suit in this behalf expended and the Defendants in mercy,&c.
        Plaintiff's costs   180 lbs tobacco @ 1 1/2   ]
                              60 lbs tobacco @ 1 1/4   ] p pound & $8.19
        Execution issued

        Lewis & Bingham v Edwards's Admrs..
        The Commonwealth of Virginia to the Sheriff of Prince William County, Greeting; We command you that you take WILLIAM POWELL and BENJAMIN EDWARDS, Administrators of BENJAMIN EDWARDS, deceased, if they be found within your Bailiwick and them safely keep so that you have their bodies before the Judges of the District Court to be held at the Town of DUMFRIES at the next Court to answer MORDECAI LEWIS and WILLIAM BINGHAM, Assignees of WILLIAM HARTSHORNE, who was Assignee of GIRDON CHAPIN & CO., of a Plea for Debt for fifty six pounds, sixteen shillings and eight pence, damage ten pounds,

p.   Lewis & Bingham v Edwards's Admrs.
178   And have then there this Writ. Witness GEORGE BROOKE, Clerk of the
        Court at DUMFRIES the 10th day of April in the 14th year of the Common-
wealth A. D. 1790

                        G. BROOKE, C. D. D. C.

        For Debt due by Penal Bill
        Executed on WILLIAM POWELL. BENJAMIN EDWARDS no Inhabitant
                        Y. PEYTON, D. Sheriff

        [blank] County, to wit
        MORDECAI LEWIS & COMPANY, Assignees of WILLIAM HARTSHORNE
who was Assignee of GURDON CHAPIN & COMPANY, complains of WILLIAM
POWELL and BENJAMIN EDWARDS, Administrators of BENJAMIN EDWARDS,
SENR. deceased, in custody &c., of a Plea that they render unto them the just and
full sum of fifty six pounds, sixteen shillings and eight pence in silver dollars at six
shillings each and other gold or silver in proportion which from them they unjustly
detain for that whereas BENJAMIN EDWARDS, SENR. in his life time, to wit, on
the eighth day of November in the year one thousand seven hundred and eighty seven
at the Parish of [blank] and County aforesaid by his certain Bill Obligatory sealed with
his seal and to the Court now here shewn the date whereof is on the same day and
year did promise to pay unto GURDON CHAPIN & CO. or order in three months
from the date of the Bill Obligatory the sum of twenty eight pounds, eight shillings and
four pence like money as above for value received and to the payment well and truly
to be made he bound himself his heirs and Execuors in the penal sum of fifty six
pounds, sixteen shillings and eight pence like money and the Plaintiffs in fact say that
BENJAMIN EDWARDS, SENR. in his life time did not nor did the Defendants or
either of them after his death pay unto GURDON CHAPIN & CO. or to either of
them the sum of twenty eight pounds eight shillings and four pence or any penny
thereof within three months from

p.   Lewis & Bingham v Edwards's Admrs.
179   date of the Bill Obligatory which ought to have been paid according to the
        form and effect of the Bill Obligatory whereby an action accrued to GURDEN
CHAPIN & CO., to demand and have of BENJAMIN in his life time and after his
death of the Defendants, the sum of fifty six pounds, sixteen shillings and eight pence
and whereas GURDEN CHAPIN & CO. afterwards, to wit, on the 18th of February
1790 at the Parish and County aforesaid, BENJAMIN being then dead and the sum
of fifty six pounds, sixteen shillings and eight pence and every penny being thereof
then and there due and unpaid assigned the Bill Obligatory to WILLIAM HARTS-
HORNE by their certain writing indorsed on the back of the Bill Obligatory signed
with their proper hands and names by means whereof WILLIAM HARTSHORNE
became entitled to receive the sum of fifty six pounds, sixteen shillings and eight
pence, the penalty of the Bill, and the same being so due and wholly unpaid to
WILLIAM, he WILLIAM afterwards, to wit, the fifth day of April in the year last
mentioned at the Parish and County aforesaid by their certain Note in writing
indorsed on the back of the Bill Obligatory with his proper hand and name thereto
assigned the Bill Obligatory to MORDECAI LEWIS & COMPANY which Company
consists of MORDECAI LEWIS and WILLIAM BINGHAM, for value received, of

of which several Assignments, the Defendants afterwards, to wit, the day year and place last mentioned had notice by which and by force of the Act of Assembly in such cases made and provided action accrued to Plaintiffs to demand and have of the Defendants the sum of fifty six pounds, sixteen shillings and eight pence, yet the Defendants altho thereto often required, the sum of money or any penny thereof to the Plaintiffs or either of them have not yet nor hath either of them paid but the same to them or to either of them to pay they have each of them hath altogether and they do and each of them doth still refuse to the damage of the Plaintiffs [blank] therefore they bring suit,&c.

SIMMS for the Plaintiffs

Pledges &c. J. Doe & R. Roe

p.   <u>Lewis & Bingham v Edwards's Admrs.</u>
180   June 1790   Common Order against POWELL and abates against
                              other
        July 1790   Common Order confirmed

I promise to pay to GURDEN CHAPIN & CO. or order in three months from this date the sum of twenty eight pounds, eight shillings and four pence in silver dollars at six shillings each or other gold or silver in proportion for value received, to which payment I bind myself my heirs and Executors in the penal sum of fifty six pounds, sixteen shillings and eight pence like money, Witness my hand and seal this eighth day of November 1787

AQUILA BROWNE   BEN: EDWARDS, SENR [seal]
Pay the within to Mr. WILLIAM HARTSHORNE February 18th 1790
                                     GURDEN CHAPIN & CO.
I assign the within Note to MORDECAI LEWIS & CO., for value received April 5th 1790.

WM. HARTSHORNE

October 15th 1793
        MORDECAI LEWIS & WILLIAM BINGHAM,
        Assignees of WILLIAM HARTSHORNE who was
        Assignee of GURDEN CHAPIN & CO., Plaintiffs   ]
            against   ]   In Debt
        WILLIAM POWELL, Administrator of BENJAMIN   ]
        EDWARDS, SENR., deced., Defendant   ]
This day came the parties by their Attornies and the Defendant relinquishing his former Plea acknowledged the Plaintiffs's action against him; therefore it is considered by the Court that the Plaintiffs recover against the Defendant fifty six pounds, sixteen shillings and eight pence in silver dollars at six shillings each or other gold and silver in proportion, the Debt in the Declaraton mentioned, and their costs by them about their suit in this behalf expended to be levied of the goods and chattles of the deceased at the time of his death in the hands of the Defendant to be administered if so much thereof in his hands he hath but if not then costs to be levied of his own proper goods and chattles and the Defendant in mercy, &c. But this Judgment may be discharged by the payment of twenty eight pounds, eight shillings and four pence like money with Interest thereon to be computed after the rate of five per centum per

annum from the 8th day of February 1788 untill paid and the costs
     Plaintiffs's costs   165 lbs tobacco at 1 1/2]
                     60 lbs tobacco at 1 1/4] p pound & $8.38.
     Execution issued.

p.   <u>Lewis & Bingham v Thorn</u>
181   The Commonwealth of Virginia to the Sheriff of FAIRFAX County, Greeting;
     We command you that you take MICHAEL THORN if he be found within your
Bailiwick and him safely keep so that you have his body before the Judges of the
District Court to be held at the Town of DUMFRIES at the next Court to answer
MORDECAI LEWIS and WILLIAM BINGHAM, Assignees of WILLIAM HARTS-
HORNE, who was Assignee of GURDEN CHAPIN & COMPANY of a Plea of Debt
for seventy pounds, three shillings and six pence, damage ten pounds, and have then
there this Writ. Witness GEORGE BROOKE, Clerk of the Court at DUMFRIES the
10th day of April in the 14th year of the Commonwealth A. D. 1790
                             G. BROOKE, C. D. D. C
     The Debt due by Penal Bill, Bail is required   SIMMS
 ·Executed ANDREW WAILES Bail
               p. BALDWIN DADE
FAIRFAX County, to wit;
     MORDECAI LEWIS and WILLIAM BINGHAM, Assignees of WILLIAM
HARTSHORNE, who was Assignee of GURDEN CHAPIN & COMPANY, complain
of MICHAEL THORN in custody, &c. of a Plea that he render unto them the sum of
seventy pounds, three shillings and six pence which to them he owes and from them
unjustly detains for that whereas the Defendant on the thirty first day of May in the
year of our Lord one thousand seven hundred and eighty eight at the Parish of FAIR-
FAX in the County aforesaid, by his certain Bill Obligatory sealed with his seal to the
Court now here shewn, whose date is on the same day and year, did promise to pay to
GURDEN CHAPIN & COMPANY or order on demand the sum of thirty five pounds,
one shilling and six pence with lawful Interest for the same in silver dollars at six shillings each for value received, to which payment he bound himself his Executors and
Administrators in the penal sum of seventy pounds, three shillings and six pence like
money as above directed and the Plaintiffs in fact sy that the Defendant did not pay
to GURDEN CHAPIN & COMPANY or to either of them the sum of thirty five
pounds, one shilling and six pence when required to wit on the [blank] day of [blank] in
the year [blank] at the Parish and County aforesaid

p.   <u>Lewis & Bingham v Thorn</u>
182   at which time the same ought to have been paid according to the tenor and
     effect of the Bill by means whereof action accrued to GURDEN CHAPIN &
COMPANY to demand and have of the Defendant the sum of seventy pounds, three
shillings six pence and whereas GURDEN CHAPIN & CO. afterwards, to wit, the
16th day of February 1790 at the Parish and County aforesaid, the seventy pounds,
three shillings and six pence and every penny thereof being then and there due and
unpaid by their certain writing endorsed on teh back of the Bill in their proper hands

and names thereto subscribed assigned the Bill to WILLIAM HARTSHORNE, whereby WILLIAM HARTSHORNE became intitled to receive the sum of seventy pounds, three shillings and six pence which being then and there due and wholly unpaid to WILLIAM, he WILLIAM afterwards, to wit, the 5th day of April 1801 at the Parish and County aforesaid by his Note in writing endorsed on the back of the Bill signed with his proper hand and name assigned the last mentioned sum of money to MORDECAI LEWIS & COMPANY, which Company consists of MORDECAI LEWIS and WILLIAM BINGHAM, of which several Assignments the Defendant the day year and place last mentioned had notice by virtue whereof and by force of the Act of Assembly in such cases made and provided, action accrued to the Plaintiffs to demand and have of the Defendant the sum of money last mentioned, yet the Defendant altho often required &c. the sum of money to the Plaintiffs or to either of them hath not paid but the same to them to pay hath altogether refused and still doth refuse to the damage of the Plaintiffs [blank] pounds and therefore they bring suit &c

SIMMS for the Plaintiffs

Pledges &c. J. Doe & R. Roe
June 1790   Common Order against Defendant and Security
July 1790   Common Order confirmed

KNOW ALL MEN by these presents that we MICHAEL THORN and ANDREW WAILES of the Town of ALEXANDRIA and County of FAIRFAX are held and firmly bound unto ROBERT TOWNSHEND HOOE, Sheriff of FAIRFAX County

p.   Lewis & Bingham v Thorn
183   in the just and full sum of one hundred forty eight shillings current money of Virginia to be paid to ROBERT T. HOOE his Executors, Administrators or assigns to which payment well and truly to be made we bind ourselves and each of us our and each of our heirs Executors and Administrators jointly and severally firmly by these presents. Sealed with our seals and dated this thirteenth day of April 1790

Whereas MORDECAI LEWIS and WILLIAM BINGHAM, Assignees of WILLIAM HARTSHORNE, who was Assignee of GURDEN CHAPIN, hath sued forth against MICHAEL THORN out of the District Court of DUMFRIES a Writ of capias ad respondendum in a Plea of Debt for seventy pounds, three shillings and six pence, damage ten pounds, directed unto the Sheriff of FAIRFAX County which hath been executed upon MICHAEL THORN.

Now the Condition of the above obligation is such that if the above bound MICHAEL THORN do make his personal appearance at the District Court to be held for the District at the Courthouse in DUMFRIES on the twelfth day of May and do then and thre abide by fulfill and perform such Order as by the Court shall be made in the action, and do not depart from the Court till the same shall be performed, then the above Obligation to be void or else to remain in full force power and virtue in Law Signed & delivered in presence of
CLEON MOORE   MICHAEL THORN   [seal]
                                         ANDREW WALES   [seal]

I promise to pay GURDEN CHAPIN & CO. or order on demand thirty five pounds, one shilling and six pence with lawful Interest for the same in silver dollars at six shillings each or other silver or gold in proportion for value received, to which payment I bind myself my heirs Executors and Administrators in the penal sum of seventy pounds, three shillings and six pence like money. Witness my hand and seal this first day of May in the year one thousand seven hundred and eighty eight Sealed and delivered in the presence of

JAMES CHAPMAN   MICHAEL THORN [seal]

p.   Lewis & Bingham v Thorn
184   Pay the within to Mr. WILLIAM HARTSHORNE
                              GURDEN CHAPMAN & CO.
                                   February 16th 1790
       I assign the within Note to MORDECAI LEWIS & CO. April 5th 1790
                              WM. HARTSHORNE

       The following belongs to the suit LEWIS & BINGHAM v SLAUGHTER
Recorded page 192.
       Mrs. ANNE SLAUGHTER to WM. HARTSHORNE, Dr.

Date		Description	£ s d
1786 Feby. 17.		To your note due this day for	L 41...11.....1 1/2
	Cr	By short Credit on 12 1/4 bushels Wheat Sept 15th 1785 of 6d p bushel	6.....1 1/2
	Dr.	To Interest on ballance to 13th November say 8 months & 27 days @ 5 p cent p annum	1...10.....7 1/2
Nov. 13th	Cr	By 15 45/60 Bushels Wheat @ 5/ for 60 lbs	3...18.....9
		To Interest on ballance to 14 Sept 1787, 10 months & 1 day @ 5 p cent	1...12.....5
1787 Sept 14	Cr.	By 14 47/60 bushels Wheat at 5/ for 60 lbs	3....13...11
	Dr.	To Interest on ballance to Sept 8th 1788 11 months & 25 days at 5 p cent	1...16.....4
1788 Sept 8	Cr.	By 10 1/2 bushels Wheat net 53 3/4 is 9 22/60 bushels @ 4/ 6 for 60 lbs	2.....2.....1 1/2
	Dr	To Interest to Sept 18 10 days @ 5 p cent	0.....1.....0
Sept 18	Cr	By 12 1/2 bushels Wehat net 53 1/2 is 11 8/60 bushels @ 4/6 for 60 lbs	2...10.....1
	Dr	To Interest to 9th October is 21 days @ 5 p cent	0.....1...11 1/2
Oct. 9	Cr	By 15 1/2 bushels Wheat net 53 1/2 lbs is 13 49/60 p bushel @ 4/6 p 60 lbs.	3.....2.....5
	Dr	To Interest on ballance to 19th October is 10 days @ 5 p cent p annum	0...10.....0
Oct 19	Cr	By 16 bushels Wheat net 54 1/2 is 14 32/60 @ 4/6	3.....4.....7 1/2
	Dr	To Interest on ballance to 21st Octo. is 2 days @ 5 p cent	0.....0.....1 1/2
Oct 21	Cr	By 16 1/2 bushels Wheat net 53 lbs is 14 32/60 bushels at 4/6 p 60 lbs.	3.....4.....7 1/2
1789 April 15	Dr	To 20 bushels Shorts from Colo. GILPIN's Mill	1.,,..0...0
19		To 5 bushels Salt 3/ 1 Ship Stuff 20/ 1...15...0	2...15.....0
1789 Sept 9	Dr	To Interest from 21st October 1788 to this time 10 months, 10 days @ 5 p cent	1....4.....9
		Due WH	L 28...11.....6

p.   Lewis & Bingham v Thorn
185   October 15, 1793
       MORDECAI LEWIS & WILLIAM BINGHAM, Assignees of

WILLIAM HARTSHORNE, who was Assignee of GURDEN
CHAPIN & COMPANY, Plaintiffs]
     against] In Debt
MICHAEL THORN, Defendant]

This day came the parties by their Attornies and the Defendant relinquishing his former Plea acknowledged Plaintiffs's action against him; therefore it is considered by the Court that the Plaintiffs recover against the Defendant seventy pounds, three shillings and six pence in silver dollars at six shillings each or other silver or gold in proportion, the Debt in the Declaration mentined, and their costs by them about their suit in this behalf expended, and the Defendant in mercy,&c., But this Judgment may be discharged by the payment of thirty two pounds, one shilling and six pence like money with Interest thereon to be computed after the rate of five per centum per annum from the first day of May 1788 untill paid and the costs

    Plaintiffs's costs   150 lbs. tobacco @ 1 1/3]
                      60 lbs. tobacco @ 1 1/4   ] p pound & $8.38
    Execution issued

Lewis & Bingham v Love

    The Commonwealth of Virginia to the Sheriff of Prince William County, Greeting, We command you that you take JOHN LOVE if he be found within your Bailiwick and him safely keep so that you have his body before the Judges of the District Court to be holden at the Town of DUMFRIES at the next Court to answer MORDECAI LEWIS and WILLIAM BINGHAM, Assigness of WILLIAM HARTS- HORNE who was Assignee of GURDEN CHAPIN & CO. of a Plea of Debt for forty eight pounds and four pence, damage ten pounds, And have then there this Writ. Witness GEORGE BROOKE, Clerk of the Court at DUMFRIES the 10th day of April in the 14th year of the Commonwealth A. D. 1790
                          G. BROOKE, C. D. D. C.
    For Debt due by Penal Bill, Bail is required
    Executed   GEORGE GRAY TYLER

p.   Lewis & Bingham v Love
186   Prince William County, to wit
    MORDECAI LEWIS & WILLIAM BINGHAM, Assignees of WILLIAM HARTSHORNE who was Assignee of GURDEN CHAPIN & COMPANY complain of JOHN LOVE in custody, of a Plea that he render unto them the just and full sum of thirty eight pounds and four pence in silver dollars at six shillings each or other silver or gold in proportion which to them he owes and from them unjustly detains for that whereas the Defendant on the third day of May one thousand seven hundred and eighty eight at the Parish of [blank] and County aforesaid by his certai Bill Obligatory sealed with his seal and to the Court now here shewn, the date whereof is on the same day and year aforesaid did promise to pay to GURDEN CHAPIN & COMPANY or order on demand the sum of nineteen pounds and two pence like money as above for value received and to the payment well and truly to be made he bound himself his heirs Executors and Administrators in the penal sum of thirty eight pounds and four

pence like money and the Plaintiffs in fact say that the Defendant did not pay to GURDEN CHAPIN & COMPANY or to either of them the sum of nineteen pounds and two pence when required to wit on the [blank] day of [blank] in the year [blank] at the Parish and County aforesaid at which time the same ought to have been paid according to the form and effect of the Bill Obligatory by means whereof action hath accrued to GURDEN CHAPIN & COMPANY to demand and have of the Defendant the sum of thirty eight pounds and four pence, And whereas GURDEN CHAPIN & COMPANY afterwards, to wit, the sixteenth day of February in the year one thousand seven hundred and ninety at the Parish and County aforesaid the sum of thirty eight pounds and four pence and every penny thereof being then and there due and unpaid to GURDEN CHAPIN & COMPANY by their certain Attorney endorsed on the back of the Bill Obligatory with their proper hands and names thereto subscribed assigned the Bill Obligatory to WILLIAM HARTSHORNE by means whereof WILLIAM HARTSHORNE became entitled to receive the sum of thirty eight pounds and four pence, the penalty of the Bill Obligatory and the same being so

p.   Lewis & Bingham v Love.
187   due and wholly unpaid to WILLIAM HARTSHORNE, he, WILLIAM HARTS-
        HORNE afterwards, to wit, the fifth day of April in the year last mentioned at the Parish and County aforesaid by his certain Note in writing endorsed on the back of the Bill Obligatory with his proper hand and name thereto subscribed assigned the Bill Obligatory to MORDECAI LEWIS & COMPANY, which Company consists of MORDECAI LEWIS and WILLIAM BINGHAM, for value received of which several assignments the Defendant the day year and place last mentioned had notice by which and by force of the Act of Assembly in such cases made and provided action accrued to the Plaintiffs to demand and have of the Defendant the sum of thirty eight pounds and four pence, yet the Defendant altho hereto often required &c. the sum of money or any part thereof to the Plaintiffs or to either of them hath not paid but the same to them or either of them to pay hath altogether refused and still doth refuse to the damage of the Plaintiffs [blank] pounds, therefore they bring suit &c.

                              SIMMS for the Plaintiff

Pledges &c.] J. Doe & R. Roe
June 1790   Common Order against Defendant & Security
July 1790   Common Order confirmed
October 1790   Common Order set aside and payment joined

        Memorandum; That on the 23d day of September in the year of our Lord one thousand seven hundred and ninety SAMUEL LOVE of the County of Prince William appeared before me, FRANCIS TRIPLETT, Gentleman, one of the Justices of the Peace for FAUQUIER County and undertook for JOHN LOVE at the suit of LEWIS & BINGHAM, Assignees of WILLIAM HARTSHORNE & COMPANY in an action of Debt now depending in the District Court held at DUMFRIES that in case JOHN LOVE shall be cast in the suit he, JOHN LOVE, will pay and satisfy the condemnation of the Court or render his body to Prison in Execution for the same or that he, SAMUEL LOVE, will do it for him, Given under my hand and seal the day and year aforesaid

                              FRANCIS TRIPLETT   [seal]

p.   Lewis & Bingham v Love
188   I promise to pay to GURDEN CHAPIN & CO. or order on demand nineteen
        pounds and two pence [in silver dollars at six shillings each or other silver or
gold in proportion] for value received, to which payment I bind myself my heirs
Executors and Administrators in the penal sum of thirty eight pounds and four pence
like money, Witness my hand and seal this third day of May in the year one thousand
seven hundred and eighty eight
Sealed and delivered in presence of
        AQUILA BROWNE   JOHN LOVE   [seal]

            Pay the within to Mr. WILLIAM HARTSHORNE
                                GURDEN CHAPIN & CO.
                                February 16th 1790
        I assign the within Note to MORDECAI LEWIS & CO. for value received
                April 5th 1790   WM: HARTSHORNE
October 15th 1793
        MORDECAI LEWIS & WILLIAM BINGHAM,
        Assignee of WILLIAM HARTSHORNE, who was
        Assignee of GURDEN CHAPIN & COMPANY, Plaintiffs]
                against   ]   In Debt
        JOHN LOVE, Defendant   ]
     This day came the parties by their Attornies and the Defendant relinquishing his
former Plea acknowledged the Plaintiffs's action against him; therefore it is considered by the Court that the Plaintiffs recover against the Defendants thirty eight
pounds and four pence in silver dollars at six shillings each or other silver or gold in
proportion, the Debt in the Declaration mentioned, and their costs by them about
their suit in this behalf expended, and the Defendant in mercy, &c., But this Judgment may be discharged by payment of nineteen pounds and two pence like money
with Interest thereon to be computed after the rate of five per centum per annum
from the third day of May 1788 untill paid and the costs
        Plaintiffs's costs   150 lbs tobacco @ 1 1/2]
                              60 lbs tobacco @ 1 1/4] p pound & $ 8.38.
        Execution issued

p.   Robinson, Sanderson & Rumney v Littlejohn
189   The Commonwealth of Virginia to the Sheriff of LOUDOUN County Greeting.
        We command you that you take JOHN LITTLEJOHN if he be found within
your Bailiwick and him safely keep so as to have his body before the Judges of the
District Court to be held at the Town of DUMFRIES at the next Court to answer
ROBINSON, SANDERSON and RUMNEY of a Plea of Debt for one hundred pounds,
seventeen shillings Virginia currency, damage thirty pounds, and have then there this
Writ. Witness GEORGE BROOKE, Clerk of the Court at DUMFRIES the 10th day
of April in the 14th year of the Commonwealth A. D. 1790
                        G. BROOKE, C. D. D. C.
        For Debt due by Bond Executed OSBORN KING, D. Sh.

KNOW ALL MEN by these presents that we JOHN LITTLEJOHN and OSBORN KING of LOUDOUN County are held and firmly bound unto JAMES COLEMAN, Gentleman, Sheriff of LOUDOUN County, in the just sum of two hundred pounds, fourteen shillings Virginia currency, to the which payment well and truly to be made to JAMES COLEMAN, his heirs Executors Administrators or assigns we bind ourselves our heirs Executors and Administrators jointly and severally and firmly by these presents; Sealed with our seals and dated the 10th day of May 1790

THE CONDITION of the above Obligation is such that whereas a Writ has been served upon the above bound JOHN LITTLEJOHN returnable to the District Court of Dumfries; Now if JOHN LITTLEJOHN shall make his appearance at the District Court to be held at the Town of DUMFRIES the the next Court to answer ROBINSON, SANDERSON and RUMNEY of a Plea of Debt for one hundred pounds, seventeen shillings Virginia currency and damage, thirty pounds, and to abide by and perform the Order and Judgment of the Court and not to depart without leave, then the above Obligation to be void else to remain in full force and virtue

Sealed and delivered in the presence of

TIMOTHY HOWELL   JOHN LITTLEJOHN   [seal]
                                  OSBORN KING   [seal]

p.   Robinson, Sanderson & Rumney v Littlejohn
190   LOUDOUN County, to wit

ROBINSON, SANDERSON & RUMNEY complain of JOHN LITTLEJOHN in custody and so forth of a Plea that he render unto them the sum of one hundred pounds, seventeen shillings Virginia currency which to them he owes and frm them unjustly detains for that, to wit, that whereas the Defendant on the sixteenth day of May in the year 1788 at the Parish of [blank] in the County aforesaid acknowledged himself to be held and firmly bound to the Plaintiffs in the sum of one hundred pounds, seventeen shillings Virginia currency, to be paid to the Plaintiffs when he should be afterwards required by his certain Writing Obligatory sealed with his seal and to the Court have now shewn, the date whereof is the same day and year aforesaid; Nevertheless the Defendant though often afterwards required hath not paid the sum of one hundred pounds, seventeen shillings Virginia currency to the Plaintiffs but hath hitherto refused and still doth refuse to pay the same to them to their damage [blank] pounds, therefore they bring this suit, &c.

CHARLES LEE for Plaintiffs

Pledges of Prosecution
John Doe & Richard Roe
June 1790   Common Order against Defendant and Security
July 1790   Common Order confirmed
October 1790   Payment for Security and set aside

KNOW ALL MEN by these presents tht I JOHN LITTLEJOHN of Town of LEESBURG, LOUDOUN County, State of Virginia, am held and firmly bound unto ROBINSON, SANDERSON and RUMNEY of ALEXANDRIA, State aforesaid in the full and just sum of one hundred pounds, seventeen shillings Virginia currency to be paid under ROBINSON, SANDERSON & RUMNEY their certain Attorney, Executors Admiistrators or assigns, to the which payment well and truly to be made and done I bind myself

p.   Robinson, Sanderson & Rumney v Littlejohn
191   my heirs Executors and Administrators and every of them firmly by these
       presents, sealed with my seal dated this sixteenth of May in the year of our
Lord one thousand seven hundred and eighty eight
       THE CONDITION of the above Obligation is such that if the above bound JOHN
LITTLEJOHN do and shall well and truly pay or cause to be paid unto ROBINSON,
SANDERSON & RUMNEY their certain Attorney Executors Administrators or
assigns the full and just sum of fifty pounds, eight shillings and six pence half penny
Virginia currency in silver dollars at six shillings each or in silver or gold by weight at
five shillings and four pence p penny weight on demand with Interest from the date
hereof for the same, then the above Obligation to be void else to remain in full force
and virtue in Law
Sealed and delivered in the presence of
       THOMAS EDWARDS   JOHN LITTLEJOHN   [seal]
       GEORGE BENTLEY
       1788 May 16th. Received from Mr. JOHN LITTLEJOHN three pounds,
eighteen shillings in part of the within Bond   L. 3...18.....0.
                              JOHN RUMNEY
       July 30th. Received on hogshead tobacco 1179 lbs @ 22/   12...19.....4
       1789 February 27th Received three pounds in part of the
              within Bond   3.....0.....0
       June 10th 1789 Received three pounds, ten shillings cash   3...10.....0
                                                               L   23.....7.....4
       November 5th 1789. Received one pound, four shillings
              currency on account   1.....4.....0
                                                               L   24...11.....4
                       W. HODGSON, Attorney in fact for R. S. R.
       1789. By Saddler's work omitted   12.....6
October 15, 1793
       ROBINSON, SANDERSON & RUMNEY, Plaintiffs   ]
              against   ]   In Debt
       JOHN LITTLEJOHN, Defendant   ]
This day came the parties by their Attornies and the Defendant

p.   Robinson, Sanderson & Rumney v Littlejohn
192   relinquishing his former Plea acknowledged Plaintiffs's action against him;
       therefore it is considered by the Court that Plaintiffs recover against the De-
fendant one hundred pounds, seventeen shillings Virginia currency, the Debt in the
Declaration mentioned, and their costs by them about their suit in this behalf expended and the Defendant in mercy, &c., But this Judgment may be discharged by
the payment of fifty pounds, eight shillings and six pence half penny Virginia currency
in silver dollars at six shillings each or in gold at five shillings and four pence p penny
weight with Interest thereon to be computed after the rate of five per centum per
annum from the sixteenth day of May 1788 untill paid and the costs;
       The Defendant is to have credit for three pounds, sixteen shillings paid the

16th May 1788; for twelve pounds, nineteen shillings and four pence paid 30th July 1788; for three pounds paid the 27th of February 1789; for three pounds, ten shillings paid the 10th day of June 1789; for one pound, four shillings paid the fifth day of November 1789 and for twelve shillings and six pence paid in the year 1789.

Plaintiffs's costs   150 lbs tobacco @ 1 1/2   ]
                        60 lbs tobacco @ 1 1/4   ] p pound & $7.97

Execution issued

Lewis & Bingham v Slaughter

The Commonwealth of Virginia to the Sheriff of FAIRFAX County, Greeting, We command you that you take ANNE SLAUGHTER if she be found within your Bailiwick and her safely keep so that you have her body before the Judges of the District Court to be held at the Town of DUMFRIES at the next Court to answer MORDECAI LEWIS & WILLIAM BINGHAM, Assignees of WILLIAM HARTS-HORNE & COMPANY of a Plea of Debt for eighty three pounds, two shillings and three pence currency, damage ten pounds, and have then there this Writ. Witness GEORGE BROOKE, Clerk of the Court at DUMFRIES the 10th day of April in the 14th year of the Commonwealth A. D. 1790

G. BROOKE, C. D. D. C.

p   Lewis & Bingham v Slaughter
193   For Debt by Penal Bill, Bail is required
                              SIMMS
         Executed BUCKNER STITH Appearance Bail
                  CHARLES TURNER, D. S.

KNOW ALL MEN by these presents that we ANN SLAUGHTER and BUCKNER STITH are held and firmly bound unto ROBERT TOWNSHEND HOOE, Gentleman, Sheriff of FAIRFAX County, in the just and full sum of one hundred seventy six pounds, four shillings current money of Virginia to be paid unto ROBERT T. HOOE his Executors Administrators or assigns, to which payment well and truly to be made be bind ourselves and each of us our and each of our heirs Executors and Administrators jointly and severally by these presents, Sealed with our seals and dated this 7th day of May 1790

Whereas MORDECAI LEWIS and WILLIAM BINGHAM, Assignees of WILLIAM HARTSHORNE & COMPANY hath issued forth against ANN SLAUGH-TER out of the District Court of DUMFRIES a writ of capias ad respondendum in a Plea of Debt for eighty three pounds, damage ten pounds, directed unto the Sheriff of the County of FAIRFAX which has been executed upon ANN SLAUGHTER;

Now the Condition of the above Obligation is such that the above bound ANN SLAUGHTER do make her personal appearance at the next Court to be held for the District at the Courthouse in DUMFRIES on the twelfth day of May and do then and there abide by fulfill and perform such Orders as by the Court shall be made in the action and do not depart from the Court till the same shall be performed, then the above Obligation to be void or else to remain in full force power and virtue in Law

Signed and delivered in the presence of
CHARLES TURNER   .   ANN SLAUGHTER   [seal]
                              BUCKNER STITH   [seal]

p.   Lewis & Bingham v Slaughter
194   MORDECAI LEWIS & WILLIAM BINGHAM, Assignees of WILLIAM
        HARTSHORNE & COMPANY, complain of ANN SLAUGHTER in custody,
&c., of a Pea that she render unto thm the just and full sum of eighty three pounds,
two shillings and three pence currency which to them she owes and from them unjustly detains for that whereas the Defendant on the seventeenth day of November in the
year one thousand seven hundred and eighty five at the Parish of FAIRFAX in the
County aforesaid by her certain Bill Obligatory sealed with her seal and to the Court
how here shewn, the date whereof is the dame day and year aforesaid, did promise to
pay to WILLIAM HARTSHORNE & COMPANY or order on the seventeenth day of
February next ensuing the date thereof the sum of forty one pounds, eleven shillings
and one penny half penny for value received; to the payment well and truly to be
made she bound herself her heirs Executors and Administrators in the penal sum of
eighty three pounds, two shillings and three pence, and the Plaintiffs in fact say tht
the Defendant did not pay to WILLIAM HARTSHORNE & COMPANY or to either of
them the sum of forty one pounds, eleven shillings and one penny half penny on the
seventeenth day of February which to him on the seventeenth day she ought to have
paid according to the form and effect of the Bill Obligatory whereby an action accrued
to WILLIAM HARTSHORNE & COMPANY to demand and have of the Defendant
the sum of eighty three pounds, two shillings and three pence; whereupon WILLIAM
HARTSHORNE & COMPANY afterwards, to wit, the fifth day of April in the year
one thousand seven hundred and ninety at the Parish and County aforesaid the sum
of eighty three pounds, two shillings and three pence and every penny thereof being
then and

p.   Lewis & Bingham v Slaughter
195   there due and unpaid assigned the Bill Obligatory to MORDECAI LEWIS and
        COMPANY which Company consists of MORDECAI LEWIS & WILLIAM
BINGHAM, for value received by his certain writing endorsed on the back of the Bill
Obligatory signed with the proper hand and name of WILLIAM HARTSHORNE for
WILLIAM HARTSHORNE & COMPANY of which assignment the Defendant the
day year and place last mentioned had notice by means whereof and by force of the
Act of Assembly in such cases made and provided action accrued to the Plaintiffs to
demand and have of the Defendant the sum of eighty three pounds, two shillings and
three pence yet the Defendant altho thereto often required the sum of eighty three
pounds, two shillings and three pence or any penny thereof hath not paid to the
Plaintiffs or to either of them but the same to them or either of them to pay hath
altogether refused and still doth refuse to the damage of the Plaintiffs [blank] pounds,
and therefore they bring suit, &c.

                              SIMMS for the Plaintiffs
Pledges &c.] J. Doe & R. Roe
June 1790   Common Order against Defendant & Security
July 1790   Common Order confirmed

I promise to pay to WILLIAM HARTSHORNE & COMPANY or order on the seventeenth day of February next the sum of forty one pounds, eleven shillings and one penny half penny currency for value received, to which payment I bind myself my heirs Executors and Administrators in the penal sum of eighty three pounds, two shillings and three pence currency. Witness my hand and seal this seventeenth day of November in the year one thousand seven hundred and eighty five
Sealed and delivered in the presence of
    JOHN BEALLE   ANN SLAUGHTER   [seal]
[On margin: See the amount of this Note recorded page 184.]
    We assign the within Note to MORDECAI LEWIS & CO for value received
April 5th 1790   WILLIAM HARTSHORNE
          for WILLIAM HARTSHORNE & CO.

p.   Lewis & Bingham v Slaughter
196   MORDECAI LEWIS & WILLIAM BINGHAM, Assignees of   ]
WILLIAM HARTSHORNE & COMPANY, Plaintiffs   ]
        against   ] In Debt
    ANN SLAUGHTER, Defendant   ]
  This day came the parties by their Attornies and the Defendant relinquishing her former Plea acknowledged the Plaintiffs's action against her; therefore it is considered by the Court that the Plaintiffs recover against the Defendant eighty three pounds, two shillings and three pence currency, the Debt in the Declaration mentioned and their costs by them about their suit in this behalf expended and the Defendant in mercy, &c., But this Judgment may be discharged by the payment of forty one pounds, eleven shillings and one penny half penny with Interest thereon to be computed after the rate of five per centum per annum from the 17th day of February 1786 till paid and the costs
    Plaintiff's costs   150 lbs tobacco @ 1 1/2]
                60 lbs tobacco @ 1 1/4] p pound. & $8.38.
  Execution issued

    Gwatkin v Brent
  The Commonwealth of Virginia to the Sheriff of Prince William County, Greeting; We command ou that you take GEORGE BRENT if he be found within your Bailiwick and him sefely keep so that you have his body before the Judges of the District Court to be held at the Town of DUMFRIES at the next Court to answer JAMES GWATKIN of a Plea of Trespass upon the Case, damage one hundred pounds and have then there this Writ. Witness GEORGE BROOKE, Clerk of the Court at DUMFRIES the [blank] day of [blank] in the 14th year of the Commonwealth A. D. 1790
          G. BROOKE, C. D. D. C.
  For deceiving the Plaintiff in the Sale of a Negroe, no Bail required
  Executed   JAMES TRIPLETT, D. C.

p.   Gwatkin v Brent
197   Prince William, to wit
    JAMES GWATKIN complains of GEORGE BRENT in custody &c. for this, to wit that the Defendant the [blank] day of [blank] in the year of our Lord one thousand seven hundred and eighty nine at the Parish of [blank] in the County aforesaid being possessed of a certain Negroe man slave named Harry, he the Defendant offered the Negroe for sale to the Plaintiff fraudently and deceitfully affirming to and assuring the Plaintiff that the Negroe belonged to the Estate of GEORGE BRENT, deceased, and that he had power and authority to sell and dispose of the Negroe and the Plaintiff in fact says that trusting to the assurance of the Defendant he then and there purchased the Negroe of the Defendant for a valuable consideration and in fact the Plaintiff says that the Negroe slave at that time did not belong to the Estate of GEORGE BRENT, deceased, and that the Defendant had no right or authority to dispose of and sell the slave says that he is injured and hath sustained damages to the value of [blank] pounds, therefore he bring suit,&c.

SIMMS for the Plaintiff

Pledges &c   ] J. Doe & R. Roe
June 1790   Common Order against Defendant
August 1790   Common Order confirmed & Inquiry
October 16th 1793

    JAMES GWATKIN, Plaintiff   ]
        against   ] In Case
    GEORGE BRENT, Defendant   ]

    This day came the Plaintiff by his Attorney and by consent the Writ of Inquiry awarded in this Cause is set aside and the Defendant by his Attorney came and acknowledged the Plaintiff's action against him for thirty six pounds, sixteen shillings and six pence damages; therefore it is considered by the Court that the Plaintiff recover against the Defendant the damages confessed and his costs by him about his suit in this behalf expended, and the Defendant in mercy, &c.

Plaintiff's costs   130 lbs tobacco @ 1 1/2]
                  60 lbs tobacco @ 1 1/4   ] p pound & $8.23

Execution issued

p.   Fairfax v Whites
198   The Commonwealth of Virginia to the Sheriff of LOUDOUN County Greeting;
    We command you that you take ROBERT WHITE and JAMES WHITE if they be found within your Bailiwick and them safely keep so that you have their bodies before the Judges of the District Court to be held at the Courthouse in the Town of DUMFRIES at next Court to answer FERDINANDO FAIRFAX of a Plea of Trespass on the Case, damage fifty pounds, and have then then this Writ; Witness GEORGE BROOKE, Clerk of the Court at DUMFRIES the 29th day of April A. D. 1793 and in the 17th year of the Commonwealth

G. BROOKE C. D. C.

    For the conversion of 200 Pine logs by the Defendant the property of the Plaintiff to the value of fifty pounds

Executed on each Defendant   WILLIAM STEPHENS, D. S. L C.
May 1793   Common Order against Defendants
June to September Continued for Declaration

Fairfax v BETZ
        The Commonwealth of Virginia to the Sheriff of LOUDOUN County, Greeting
You are hereby commanded as you have at another time been commanded to take
PETER BETZ if he be found within your Bailiwick and him safely keep so that you
have his body before the Judges of the District Court to be held at the Town of DUM-
FRIES at the next Court to answer FERDINANDO FAIRFAX of a Plea of Trespass,
damage fifty pounds, And have then there this Writ. Witness GOERGE BROOKE
Clerk of our Court at DUMFRIES the 30th day of May 1793 and in the 17th year of
the Commonwealth
                              G. BROOKE, C. D. C.
        For cutting taking and carrying away Pine logs from off the land of the Plaintiff
and also for sawing and destroying Pine logs the property of the Plaintiff
                              SWANN for Plaintiff
        Executed ISAAC LARROWE, D. Sh.
October 16th 1793

FERDINANDO FAIRFAX, Plaintiff against ROBERT WHITE & JAMES WHITE, Defendants	In Case
FERDINANDO FAIRFAX, Plaintiff against PETER BETZ, Defendant	In Trespass

        These suits are agreed, the Defendants paying costs

p.   Dick v LINDSAY
199   The Commonwealth of Virginia to the Sheriff of FAIRFAX County, Greeting
        We command you that you take WALKER LINDSAY if he be found within
your Bailiwick and him safely keep so that you have his body before the Judges of the
District Court to be held at the Town of DUMFRIES at the next Court to answer
Negroe Dick of a Plea of Trespass, Assault and Battery, damage one hundred pounds,
and have then there this Writ. Witness GEORGE BROOKE, Clerk of our Court at
DUMFRIES the 22d day of July in the 16th year of the Commonwealth A.D. 1791
                              G. BROOKE, C. D. C.
        For an Assault and Battery committed by the Defendant on the Plaintiff
                              C. SIMMS, Attorney for Plaintiff
FAIRFAX to wit.
        Negroe Dick complains of WILLIAM LINDSAY JUNR in custody &c. for this
to wit, that the Defendant on the [blank] day of [blank] in the year of our Lord one thousand seven hundred and ninety one at the Parish of Truro and County aforesaid with

force and arms to wit with sticks staves fists swords and knives an assault did make on the Plaintiff and him the Plaintiff did beat wound and evil entreat and then and there did other wrongs and injustices to the Plaintiff against the peace of the Commonwealth and to the damage of the Plaintiff [blank] pounds; wherefore he brings suit &c.

SIMMS for the Plaintiff

Pledges &c. } J. Doe & R. Roe
Octobr 1791   Declaration filed and Common Order against Defendant
November 1791   Common Order confirmed & Inquiry
December 1791   Inquiry set aside and Not Guilty joined

I do agree to pay the Clerk's charges in the suit between Dick and myself

GEORGE W. LINDSAY
October 14th 1793

Negroe Dick, Plaintiff   ]
      against   ] In Trespass Assault &
WALKER LINDSAY   ] Battery
This suit is agreed the Defendant paying the costs
      Plaintiff's costs   30 lbs. tobacco @ 1 1/2]
                                      125 lbs. tobacco @ 1 1/4] p pounds & $4.36.

[Note: In the foregoing Suit the name of the Defendant appears at Walker Lindsay, William Linday Junr. and George W. Lindsay]

p.   Armistead's Exr. v Carter's Admrs.
200   The Commonwealth of Virginia to the Sheriff of Prince William County,
      Greeting. We command you take LANDON CARTER, WORMLEY CARTER and ROBERT CARTER, Administrators of JOHN CARTER, deceased, if they be found within your Bailiwick and them safely keep so that you have their bodies before the Judges of the District Court to be held at the Town of DUMFRIES at the next Court to answer WILLIAM PEACHY, Executor of HENRY ARMISTEAD, deceased, Assignee of GEORGE FRENCH, who was Assignee of JOHN LEWIS, of a Plea of Debt for seventy pounds current money of Virginia, damage five pounds, And have then there this Writ. Witness GEORGE BROOKE, Clerk of our Court at DUMFRIES the 23d day of April in the 14th year of the Commonwealth A. D. 1790

GEORGE BROOKE, C. D. D. C.

On Bond.
      Executed on LANDON CARTER and to late to hand to be executed on WORMLEY and ROBERT CARTER.

GEORGE G. TYLER, D. Sh.

The Commonwealth of Virginia to the Sheriff of Prince William County, Greeting; We command you as we have at another time commanded you that you take ROBERT CARTER and WORMLEY CARTER, Administrators of JOHN CARTER, deceased, if they be found in your Bailiwick and them safely keep so that you have their bodies before the Judges of the District Court to be held at the Town of DUMFRIES at the next Court to answer WILLIAM PEACHY, Executor of HENRY ARMISTEAD, deceased, Assignee of GEORGE FRENCH who was Assignee of JOHN LEWIS for a Plea of Debt for seventy pounds current money of Virginia, damage five pounds, and have then there this Writ. Witness GEORGE BROOKE, Clerk of our Court at DUMFRIES the 31st day of July in the 15th year of the Commonwealth A. D. 1790

G. BROOKE C. D. C.

On Bond
Executed on WORMLEY CARTER & ROBERT CARTER
GEORGE G. TYLER, D. S.

June 1790	Common Order against LANDON & others
July 1790	Common Order confirmed
October 1790	Common Order set aside and payment joined

p.   Armistead's Exr. v Carter's Admrs.
201
November 1790-	Common Order
December 1790	Common Order confirmed
May 1791	Common Order set aside & payment joined

Prince William County, to wit.

WILLIAM PEACHY, Executor of the LastWill and Testament of HENRY ARMISTEAD, deceased, Assignee of GEORGE FRENCH, who was Assignee of JOHN LEWIS complains of [blank] Administrators of the goods and chattles of JOHN CARTER, deced., who died intestate in custody &c., of a Plea that they render unto him the sum of seventy pounds current money of Virginia which they unjustly detain from him for this, to wit, that whereas JOHN CARTER in his life time, to wit, on the fourth day of October one thousand seven hundred and eighty seven at Prince William County by his certain Writing Obligatory sealed with his seal and to the Court now here shewn, the date wheref is the same day and year aforesaid acknowledged himself to be indebted to JOHN LEWIS in the sum of seventy pounds current money of Virginia to be paid to JOHN LEWIS his certain Attorney his heirs, Executors Administrators & assigns whenever he should be thereunto required, And whereas JOHN LEWIS afterwards, that is to say, on the twenty third day of October in the year of our Lord one thousand seven hundred and eighty seven at Prince William County by his certain endorsement on the Bond directed the contents to be paid to one GEORGE FRENCH who afterwards by his endorsement on the Bond assigned the same to the Plaintiff of which several assignments JOHN CARTER in his life time then and there had notice by reason whereof and by virtue of the Act of Assembly in that case made and provided an action hath accrued to the Plaintiff to have and demand the seventy pounds, Nevertheless JOHN CARTER in his life time and the [blank] after the death of JOHN altho often requested have not paid

p.   Armistead's Exr. v Carter's Admrs.
202   nor hath either of them paid the seventy pounds to the Plaintiff but the [blank] hitherto have refused and still do refuse to pay the same to the damage of the Plaintiff five pounds and therefore he brings suit &c.

J. MINOR, JR. for Plaintiff

KNOW ALL MEN by these presents that I JOHN CARTER of the County of Prince William and State of Virginia am held and firmly bound unto JOHN LEWIS of the County of SPOTSYLVANIA and State aforesaid in the just and full sum of seventy pounds current money of Virginia to be paid to JOHN LEWIS or to his certain Attorney his heirs Executors Administrators or assigns to which payment well and truly to be made I bind myself my heirs Executors and Administrators firmly by these presents, Sealed with my seal and dated this fourth day of October 1787

THE CONDITION of the above Obligation is such that if the above bound JOHN CARTER do and shall well and truly pay or cause to be paid unto JOHN LEWIS or to his Executors, Administrators or assigns the full and just sum of thirty five pounds current specie of Virginia on or before the fifteenth day of December next ensuing, then the above Obligation to be void or else to remain in full force and virtue in Law Sealed and delivered in presence of

        JAMES NEWTON   JOHN CARTER [seal]
23 October 1787.
        For value received I assign the within Bond to Doctor GEORGE FRENCH
                                          JOHN LEWIS
        Pay the witin to Colo. WILLIAM PEACHY, Executor of HENRY
ARMISTEAD, deceased

                                          GEO: FRENCH
October 16th 1793
        WILLIAM PEACHY, Executor of HENRY ARMISTEAD,]
        deceased, Plaintiff   ]
             against   ] In Debt
        LANDON CARTER, WORMLEY CARTER and ROBERT]
        CARTER, Administrators of JOHN CARTER, deceased,]
        Defendants   ]

    This day came the parties by their Attornies and the Defendants relinquishing their former Plea acknowledged the action of the Plaintiff against

p.   Armistead's Exr. v. Carter's Admrs.
203   them, therefore it is considered by the Court that the Plaintiff recover against
        the Defendants seventy pounds current money of Virginia, the Debt in the Declaration mentioned and his costs by him about his suit in this behalf expended to be levied of the goods and chattles of the deceased at the time of his death in the hands of the Administrators to be administered if so much thereof in their hands they have if not then the costs to be levied of their own proper goods and chattles and the Defendants in mercy, &c., But this Judgment may be discharged by the payment of twenty three pounds, three shillings and five pence with Interest thereon to be computed after the rate of five per centum per annum from the thirteenth day of June 1788 untill paid and the costs

        Plaintiff's costs   290 lbs tobacco @ 1 1/2   ]
                             115 lbs tobacco @ 1 1/4   ] p pound & $ 6.98

Robinson & Sanderson v Graham

The Commonwealth of Virginia to the Sheriff of Prince William County, Greeting
We command you that you take ROBERT GRAHAM if to be found within your Baili-
wick and him safely keep so that you have his body before the Judges of the District
Court to be held at the Town of DUMFRIES at the next Court to answer ROBINSON
SANDERSON & COMPANY, Assignees of THOMAS LEE of a Plea of Debt for six
hundred two pounds current money, damage ten pounds, and have then there this
Writ. Witness GEORGE BROOKE, Clerk of our Court at DUMFRIES the 3d day of
May in the 14th year of the Commonwealth A D 1790
G. BROOKE, C. D. D. C.
Bond for payment of three hundred pounds, eleven shillings specie
CHARLES LEE, Attorney for Plaintiffs
Executed   COLIN CAMPBELL, D. S.
Prince William County, to wit
ROBINSON, SANDERSON and COMPANY, Assignees of THOMAS LEE,
SENR. complain of ROBERT GRAHAM in custody and so forth of a Plea that he
render to them the sum of six hundred two pounds current money of Virginia which to
them he owes and from them unjustly

p.   ### Robinson & Sanderson v Graham
204   detains for this, to wit, that whereas the Defendant on the twenty fifth day of
September in the year 1787 at the Parish of [blank] in the County aforesaid by
his certain Writing Obligatory sealed with his seal and to the court here now shewn,
the date whereof is on the same day and year aforesaid, acknowledged himself to be
held and firmly bound unto THOMAS LEE, SENR. in the sum of six hundred two
pounds current money of Virginia to be paid to hm his certain Attorney, Executors,
Administrators or assigns when he, the Defendant, should thereto be afterwards
required and whereas afterwards, to wit, on the 17th day of March in the year 1790,
at the Parish and County aforesaid, THOMAS LEE, SENR. assigned to ROBINSON,
SANDERSON & COMPANY, the Plaintiffs, the Writing Obligatory the same then
and there being and yet remaining unpaid by writing the Assignment thereupon with
his proper hand whereof the Defendant the day and year last mentioned at the Parish
and County aforesaid had notice by virtue of which premises and of the Act of Assembly in such case made an action accrued to ROBINSON, SANDERSON & COM-
PANY, Assignees of THOMAS LEE, SENR. to have and demand of the Defendant
the sum of six hundred two pounds current money, Nevertheless the Defendant hath
not paid to the Plaintiffs, Assigness as aforesaid, the sum of six hundred two pounds
or any part thereof but refuses and still doth refuse to pay the same to them to their
damage [blank] pounds, therefore they bring their suit, &c.
CHARLES LEE for Plaintiffs

Pledges of Prosecution   ]
John Doe v R. Roe   ]
     June 1790   Common Order against Defendant
     July 1790   Common Order confirmed
     October 1790   Special Bail and payment
     KNOW ALL MEN by these presents that I ROBERT GRAHAM of Prince
William County am held and firmly bound unto THOMAS LEE, SENR. of the same

County in the full and just sum of six hundred two pounds current money of Virginia to be paid unto

p.   Robinson & Sanderson v Graham
205   THOMAS LEE, SENR. his certain Attorney Executors, Administrators or
        assigns to the which payment well and truly to be made and done I bind myself
my heirs Executors and Administrators firmly by these presents, Sealed with my
seal and dated this 25th day of September in the year of our Lord one thousand seven
hundred and eighty seven
        THE CONDITION of the above Obligation is such that if the above bound
ROBERT GRAHAM do and shall well and truly pay or cause to be paid unto THO-
MAS LEE, SENR. his certain Attorney, Executors, Administrators or assigns the
full and just sum of three hundred pounds, eleven shillings specie on demand with legal
Interest for the same, then the above Obligation to be void else to remain in full force
and virtue in Law
Sealed and delivered in presence of
        LUDWELL LEE,   ROBERT GRAHAM   [seal]
        RICHARD BRENT
        I assign my right and title of the within Bond to Messrs. ROBERTSON, SANDER-
SON & CO., DUMFRIES, 17th March 1790
                                THOMAS LEE, SR.
October 16, 1793
        ROBINSON, SANDERSON & COMPANY, Assignees   ]
        of THOMAS LEE, Plaintiffs   ]
                against   ] In Debt
        ROBERT GRAHAM, Defendant   [
        This day came the parties by their Attornies and the Defendant relinquishing his
former Plea acknowledged the action of the Plaintiffs against him; therefore it is considered by the Court that the Plaintiffs recover against the Defendant six hundred
two pounds current money of Virginia, the Debt in the Declaration mentioned, and
their costs by them about their suit in this behalf expended, and the Defendant in
mercy, &c., But this Judgment may be discharged by the payment of three hundred,
eleven shillings specie with Interest thereon to be computed after the rate of five per
centum per annum from the twenty fifth day of September 1787 untill paid and the
costs
        Plaintiffs's costs   150 lbs. tobacco @ 1 1/2]
                              60 lbs. tobacco @ 1 1/4   ] p pound & $8.37.
        Execution issued

p.   Armstrong v Jones
206   The Commonwealth of Virginia to the Sheriff of LOUDOUN County, Greeting.
        We command yu that you take JOHN JONES if he be found within your Baili-
wick and him safely keep so that you have his body before the Judges of the District
Court to be held at the Town of DUMFRIES at the next Court to answer ROBERT
ARMSTRONG of a Plea of Debt for one hundred fifty pounds common currency in
Spanish milled dollars at seven shillings and six pence each of the value of one hundred seenty pounds current money, damage ten pounds, And have then there this

Writ. Witness GEORGE BROOKE, Clerk of our Court at DUMFRIES the 25th day of April in the 14th year of the Commonwealth A. D. 1790

G. BROOKE, C. D. D. C.

For money due by Bond, Bail is required

SIMMS for Plaintiff

Executed, WILLIAM JONES his Appearance Bail

JAMES JENKINS

LOUDOUN County to wit;

ROBERT ARMSTRONG complains JOHN JONES in custody &c. that he render unto him the sum of one hundred fifty pounds MARYLAND Currency of the value of one hundred twenty pounds current money of Virginia which to him he owes and from him unjustly detains for that whereas the Defendant on the twenty second day of February in the year of our Lord one thousand seven hundred and eighty five at the Parish of [blank] and County aforesaid by his certain Writing Obligatory sealed with his seal and to the Court now here shewn, the date whereof is on the same day and year aforesaid, acknowledged himself to be held and firmly bound unto the Plaintiff in the sum of one hundred fifty pounds to be paid to the Plaintiff when he should be thereunto required; Nevertheless the Defendant altho often required the sum of money or any part thereof hath not yet paid but the same to him to pay hath altogether refused and still doth refuse to the damage of the Plaintiff [blank] pounds and therefore he brings suit, &c.

SIMMS for Plaintiff

Pledges &c. J. Doe & R. Roe

p.   Armstrong v Jones
207   June 1790   Common Order against Defendant & Security
       July 1790   Common Order confirmed
       October 1790   Special Bail and Payment joined

KNOW ALL MEN by these presents that I JOHN JONES of LOUDOUN County in the Commonwealth of Virginia am held and firmly bound unto ROBERT ARMSTRONG of ST. MARY's County in the State aforesaid in the just and full sum of one hundred fifty pounds common currency in Spanish milled dollars at seven shillings and six pence each to be paid unto ROBERT ARMSTRONG his certain Attorney his heirs Executors Administrators or assigns, to the which payment well and truly to be made and done I bind myself my heirs Executors and Administrators firmly by these presents, Sealed with my seal and dated this twenty second day of February one thousand seven hundred and eighty five

THE CONDITION of the above Obligation is such that if the above bound JOHN JONES do and shall well and truly pay or cause to be paid unto ROBERT ARMSTRONG his certain Attorney his heirs Executors Administrators or assigns the just and full sum of seventy five pounds like money upon the first day of August next ensuing the date hereof with legal Interest thereon from the date hereof except the same be paid by the time limited above that then the above Obligation to be void and of no effect else to remain in full force and virtue in Law

Signed sealed and delivered in the presence of

FREDERICK BYRN   JOHN JONES

Bond February 22d 1786	75.....0.....0		
Interest to 14th November 1786	7...17.....6	82...17.....6	
November 14th 1786 Cash of ROBERT PRICE	11...15.....0	71.....2.....6	
Interest to 5th of December 1786	0.....4.....9	71.....7.....3	
December 5th 1786. my order in favor WILLIAM			
JONES	7...16.....6	63...10.....9	

p. 208	Armstrong v Jones		
	February 25th 1788, Interest	4...12.....1	68.....2...10
	Same time by Cash received	19...17.....4	48.....5.....6

The 11th day of April 1790. Came the within named ROBERT ARMSTRONG before the Subscriber, one of the Justices for SAINT MARY's County and made Oath on the Holy Evangelists of Almighty God that he had not received any part or parcel security or satisfaction for the within Bond except the sum of eleven pounds, fifteen shillings and the sum of seven pounds, sixteen shillings and six pence, and the sum of nineteen pounds, seventeen shillings and four pence being the sums as above entered and that the aforesaid sums were received in the manner and at the times above stated; sworn before

J. BISAY

October 16th 1793

ROBERT ARMSTRONG, Plaintiff	]
against	]
JOHN JONES, Defendant	]

    This day came the parties by their Attorneys and the Defendant relinquishing his former :Plea acknowledged the Plaintiff's action against him; therefore it is considered by the Court that the Plaintiff recover against the Defendant one hundred fifty pounds MARYLAND Currency of the value of one hundred twenty pounds current money of Virginia, the Debt in the Declaration mentioned, and his costs by him about his suit in this behalf expended, and the Defendant in mercy, &c., But this Judgment may be discharged by the payment of forty eight pounds, five shillings and six pence like money with Interest thereon to be computed after the rate of five per centum per annum from the twenty fifth day of February 1788 untill paid and the costs

    Plaintiff's costs   150 lbs tobacco @ 1 1/2]
                      60 lbs tobacco @ 1 1/4] p pound & $7.38
    Execution issued

p. 209   Henderson, Ferguson & Gibson v Wiatts

    The Commonwealth of Virginia to the Sheriff of Prince William County, Greeting; We command you that you take JOHN WIATT and WILLIAM EDWARD WIATT if they be found within your Bailiwick and them safely keep so that you have their bodies before the Judges of the District Court to be held at the Town of DUMFRIES of a Plea of Debt for one hundred twenty three pounds, fifteen shillings and nine pence specie, damage ten pounds, And have then there this Writ. Witness GEORGE BROOKE, Clerk of our Court at DUMFRIES the 5th day of May

in the 14the year of the Commonwealth A. D. 1790
                                              G. BROOKE, C. D. D. C.

     For Debt due on Bond, Bail is required
     I do hereby agree to be the within Defendants's Appearance Bail
Test   GEORGE G. TYLER, D. S.   ALEXANDER BROWN
     Executed on JOHN WIATT
                                              GEORGE G. TYLER, D. Sh.

Prince William County, to wit
     Messrs. HENDERSON, FERGUSON & GIBSON complain of JOHN WIATT
and WILLIAM EDWARD WIATT both of Prince William County in custody &c. of a
Plea that the Defendants render to the Plaintiffs the sum of one hundred twenty three
pounds, fifteen shillings and nine pence specie which they owe the Plaintiffs and
unjustly detain from them for that, to wit, that whereas the Defendants on the 26th
dy of September in the year of our Lord one thousand seven hundred and eighty six at
the Parish of Dettingen in the County aforesaid by their certain Writing Obligatory
sealed with the seals of the Defendants and here shewn to the Court and dated the
same day and year acknowledged themselves to be held and firmly bound to the
Plaintiffs in the sum of one hundred twenty three pounds, fifteen shillings and nine
pence specie, yet the Defendants altho often required have not yet paid the one hundred twenty three pounds, fifteen shillings and nine pence specie to the Plaintiffs but
have wholly denied and still do deny to pay it to them to the damage

p.   Henderson, Ferguson & Gibson v Wiatts
210   of ten pounds to the Plaintiffs and therefore they bring suit, &c.
                                              RICHARD BRENT for Plaintiffs

For the Plaintiffs] John Doe
Pledges &c.   ] Richard Roe
June 1790   Common Order against Defendants & Security
July 1790   Common Order confirmed
     Memorandum; That on the 11th day of May 1790 personally appeared before
me, ALEXANDER BROWN, a Justice of the Peace for the County of Prince William,
WILLIAM SKINKER and undertook for WILLIAM EDWARD WIATT at the suit of
Messrs. Henderson, Ferguson and Gibson that he should pay the costs and condem-
nation of the Court or render his body to Prison in satisfaction for the same or that
WILLIAM SKINKER would do it for him. Given under my hand and seal the date
above written
                                              ALEX: BROWN   [seal]
     KNOW ALL MEN by these presents that we JOHN WIATT and WILLIAM
EDWARD WIATT of Prince William County are held and firmly bound unto Messrs.
HENDERSON, FERGUSON & GIBSON for dealings in DUMFRIES in the full and
just sum of one hundred twenty three pounds, fifteen shillings and nine pence specie
to be paid unto Messrs. HENDERSON, FERGUSON & GIBSON their certain Attorney Executors Administrators or assigns to the which payment well and truly to be
made we bind ourselves our heirs Executors and Administrators jointly and severally
firmly by these presents, Sealed with our seals and dated this twenty sixth day of
September in the year of our Lord one thousand seven hundred and eighty six
     THE CONDITION of the above Obligation is such that if the above bound JOHN

WIATT and WILLIAM EDWARD WIATT do and shall well and truly pay or cause to be paid unto Messrs. HENDERSON, FERGUSON & GIBSON or their certain Attorney Executors Administrators or assigns the full and just sum of sixty one pounds, seventeen shillings and ten pence half penny to be paid in specie at or upon the first day of January next with lawful Interest for the same then the above Obligation to be void else to remain in full force and virtue in Law

Sealed and delivered in the presence of

| JAMES PARK | JOHN WIATT | [seal] |
| JOHN G. HESLOP | W. E. WIATT | [seal] |

p. **Henderson, Ferguson & Gibson v Wiatts**

211	Principal Debt		L	61...17.....1 1/2
	Interest on Debt from 1st January 1787 to 30th Sept. 1788			5....7 1/2
			L	67.....5.....0
1788	July 4. Paid in tobacco	5....2.....7]		
	Sept 30 Paid in do.	6.....8.....4]	11...10...11	
	Due with Interest from 30th September 1788		55...14.....1	

October 16, 1793

Messrs. HENDERSON, FERGUSON & GIBSON, Plaintiffs]
           against] In Debt
JOHN WIATT & WILLIAM EDWARD WIATT, Defendants]

This day came the parties by their Attornies and the Defendants relinquishing their former Plea acknowledged the Plaintiffs's action against them; therefore it is considered by the Court that the Plaintiffs recover against the Defendants one hundred twenty three pounds, fifteen shillings and nine pence specie, the Debt in the Declararation mentioned, and their costs by them about their suit in this behalf expended, and the Defendants in mercy, &c., But this Judgment may be discharged by the payment of fifty five pounds, fourteen shillings and one penny with Interest thereon to be computed after the rate of five per centum per annum from the thirtieth day of September 1788 untill paid and the costs

Plaintiffs's costs   180 lbs tobacco @ 1 1/2]
                   60 lbs tobacco @ 1 1/4] p pound & $ 7.10

Execution issued

Wise v Stith

The Commonwealth of Virginia to the Sheriff of FAIRFAX County, Greeting; We command you as we have before commanded you to take BUCKNER STITH if he be found within your Bailiwick and him safely keep so that you have his body before the Judges of the District Court to be held at the Town of DUMFRIES on the first day of the next Court to answer JOHN WISE of a Plea of Trespass on the Case, damage one hundred pounds, And have then there this Writ. Witness HUMPHREY BROOKE Clerk of our Court a DUMFRIES the 29th day of October in the 14th year of the Commonwealth A. D. 1789

                          H. BROOKE, C. D. D. C.

On an excepted order to pay the amount of one Note and one Bond, the

amount of which is not particularized   LOVE
     Executed   p BALDWIN DADE
     May 1790   Common Order against Defendant and Sheriff
     August 1790   Continued for Declaration
FAIRFAX, to wit

     JOHN WISE complains of BUCKNER STITH in custody, &c., to wit, that a
certain TOWNSHEND DADE on the fifteenth day of June in the year of our Lord one
thousand seven hundred and eighty six at the Parish of Fairfax in the County of
FAIRFAX, was indebted to the Plaintiff in the sum of thirty one pounds, fourteen
shillings specie Virginia currency by Bond and also in the sum of fourteen pounds,
twelve shillings by Promissory Note on which Bond and Note JOHN WISE com-
menced suis in the County Court of KING GEORGE and which suits were depending
and undetermined in the Court on the day and year aforesaid and TOWNSHEND
DADE being so indebted to the Plaintiff in consideration thereof on the day and year
aforesaid drew an order on the Defendant whereby TOWNSHEND DADE requested
the Defendant to pay unto the Plaintiff the amount of the Bond and Note with the
cost of suit which order the Defendant in consideration of the premises and of his
being at that time indebted to TOWNSHEND DADE afterwards, to wit, on the day
and year last mentioned at the Parish and County aforesaid, accepted promised and
assumed to pay unto the Plaintiff the amount of the Bond and Note and the costs of
suit; Nevertheless the Defendant not regarding his promise and assumption so made
but contriving and fraudulently intending craftily and subtlely to deceive and defraud
the Plaintiff in this particular the amount of the Bond and Note and the costs of suit
to the Plaintiff did not pay altho thereto afterwards required to wit on the day and
year last mentioned

p.   Wise v Stith
213   at the Parish and County aforesaid but the same to him to pay hitherto hath
     refused and still doth refuse to the damage of the Plaintiff [blank] pounds, and
therefore he brings suit, &c.
                            SIMMS for the Plaintiff

     Pledges &c. J. Doe & R. Roe
     November 1790   Continued for Declaration
     December 1790   Declaration, Common Order confirmed and Inquiry
October 16th 1793
     JOHN WISE, Plaintiff   ]
            against   ] In Case
     BUCKNER STITH, Defendant]
This suit abates by the death of the Defendant

     Evans v Moore
     WILLIAM EVANS, Plaintiff   ]
            against   ] In Trespass Assault & Battery
     JOHN MOORE, Defendant   ]
Discontinued being agreed by the parties

Love v Wiatt

The Commonwealth of Virginia to the Sheriff of Prince William County, Greeting; We command you that you take WILLIAM EDWARD WIATT if he be found within your Bailiwick and him safely keep so that you have his body before the Judges of the District Court at the next Court to be held at the Town of DUMFRIES to answer SAMUEL LOVE of a Plea of Debt for one hundred thirty five pounds, twelve shillings and eight pence in French English or Spanish gold at five shillings and four pence the penny weight or in silver dollars at six shillings each, damage ten pounds, and have then there this Writ. Witness HUMPHREY BROOKE, Clerk of our Court at DUMFIRES the third day of October in the 14th year of the Commonwealth A. D. 1789

                                              H. BROOKE, C. D. D. C.
Upon a Penal Bill, Bail to be required

                                              J. LOVE for Plaintiff
Copy left.

                       GEORGE GRAY TYLER, D. Sh.
The Commonwealth of Virginia to the Sheriff of Prince William County, Greeting. We command you that you attach so much of the Estate of

p.   Love v Wiatt
214   the within named WILLIAM EDWARD WIATT as will be of value sufficient to pay the within mentioined sum of one hundred thirty five pounds, twelve shillings and eight pence in French English or Spanish gold at five shillings and four pence the penny weight or in siliver dollars at six shillings each, and costs, and that you secure the same in your hands or otherwise provide that it may be forthcoming and liable for payment thereof as our Judges of our District Court at the Courthouse in DUMFRIES at the next Court shall in this part consider and have then there this Writ. Witness HUMPHREY BROOKE Clerk of our Court at DUMFRIES the 29th day of October A.D. 1789 and in the fourteenth year of the Commonwealth

                              H. BROOKE, C. D. D. C.
DUMFRIES October District Court 1789
        SAMUEL LOVE, Plaintiff   ]
             against   ]   In Debt
        WILLIAM EDWARD WIATT, Defendant   ]
    The Defendant not appearing, on the moiton of the Plaintiff by his Attorney, it is ordered that an Attachment issue against the Defendant's Estate for one hundred thirty five pounds, twelve shillings and eight pence French English or Spanish gold at five shillings and four pence the penny weight or in silver dollars at six shillings each and costs returnable to next Court

                              H. BROOKE, C. D. D. C.
        Executed on one Horse
                  GEORGE G. TYLER, D Sh.
Prince William, to wit
        SAMUEL LOVE complains of WILLIAM EDWARD WIATT in custody &c. of a Plea &c., that he render unto him the sum of one hundred thirty five pounds, twelve shillings and eight pence which to him he owes and from him unjustly detains for that whereas the Defendant upon the fourth day of January in the year of our Lord one

thousand seven hundred and eighty eight at the Parish of [blank] in the County aforesaid by his certain Bill Penal in writing signed with his own hand, sealed with his seal and here in Court produced bearing date the day and year aforesaid obliged himself his heirs Executors and Administrators to pay to the Plaintiff

p.   Love v Wiatt
215   the sum of sixty seven pounds, sixteen shillings and four pence to be paid to
         the Plaintiff on demand for the same payment well and truly to be made the Defendant by the Bill firmly bound himself his heirs Executors and Administrators in the Penal sum of one hundred thirty five pounds, twelve shillings and eight pence and the Plaintiff in fact doth aver that the Defendant the sum of sixty seven pounds, sixteen shillings and four pence unto him, the Plaintiff, on demand which he ought to have paid according to the tenor and effect of the bill whereby an action accrued to the Plaintiff to have and demand of the Defendant the sum of one hundred thirty five pounds, twelve shillings and eight pence yet the Defendant altho often required hath not yet paid the sum of one hundred thirty five pounds, twelve shillings and eight pence to the Plaintiff but the same to pay hitherto hath and still doth refuse to the damage of the Plaintiff two pounds and therefore he brings suit, &c.
                                              J. LOVE for Plaintiff

         For the Plaintiff   ] J Doe
         Pledges &c.   ] R. Roe
         October 1789   Attachment
         May 1790   Bail piece filed and oyer
         July 1790   Rule to plead
         November 1790   Continued for Plea
         December 1790   Payment
         Memorandum; That on the 11th day of May 1790 personally appeared before me, ALEXANDER BROWN, a Justice of the Peace for the County of Prince William, WILLIAM SKINKER and undertook for WILLIAM EDWARD WIATT at the suit of SAMUEL LOVE that he should pay the costs and condemnation of the Court or render his body to Prison in satisfaction for the same or that he, WILLIAM SKINKER, will do it for him; Given under my hand and seal the date above written
                                       ALEX: BROWN   [seal]
         I WILLIAM EDWARD WIATT of the County of Prince William do oblige myself my heirs Executors and Administrators to pay or cause to be paid on demand unto SAMUEL LOVE of the County of LOUDOUN or to his heirs or assigns the just sum of sixty seven pounds, sixteen

p.   Love v Wiatt
216   shillings and four pence to be paid in French, English or Spanish gold at five
         shillings and four pence the penny weight or in silver dollars at six shillings each with legal Interest thereon from the date hereof till paid it being for value received, to the which payment well and truly to be made and done I bind myself my heirs Executors and Administrators jointly and severally in the penal sum of one hundred thirty five pounds, twelve shillings and eight pence like money. In Witness whereof I have hereunto set my hand and seal the twenty fourth day of January 1788

Signed and sealed in presence of
  CHARLES C. JONES   W. E. WIATT   [seal]
October 16th 1793
      SAMUEL LOVE, Plaintiff   ]
           against   ] In Debt
      WILLIAM EDWARD WIATT, Defendant   ]
  This day came the parties by their Attornies and thereupon came a Jury, to wit

WILLIAM GUNYON	NATHANIEL TRIPLETT	SHADRACK RATCLIFFE
JOHN HEDGES	JOHN GIBSON	WILLIAM HULETT
WILLIAM BEALE	GEORGE WILLIAMS	THOMAS THORNTON
WILDMAN KINCHELOE	JOSEPH BRADY and	JOSEPH NELSON

who being elected tried and sworn the truth to speak upon the issue joined upon their
Oath do say the the Defendant hath not paid the Debt in the Declaration mentioned
as by replying the Plaintiff hath alledged and they do assess the Plaintiff's damages
by means of the detention of that Debt to one penny besides his costs; therefore it is
considered by the Court that the Plaintiff recover against the Defendant one hundred
thirty five pounds, twelve shillings and eight pence in French, English or Spanish gold
at five shillings and four pence the penny weight or in silver dollars at six shillings
each, the Debt in the Declaration mentioned, and his costs by him about his suit in
this behalf expended, and the Defendant in mercy, &c., But this Judgment may be
discharged by the payment of sixty seven pounds, sixteen shillings and four pence like
money with Interest thereon to be computed after the rate of five per centum per
annum from the 24th day of January 1788 untill paid and the damages and costs

p.   Edmonds v Blackburn
217   The Commonwealth of Virginia to the Sheriff of FAIRFAX County, Greeting;
      We command you that you take RICHARD SCOTT BLACKBURN if he be
found within your Bailiwick and him safely keep so that you have him before the
Judges of the District Court to be held at the Town of DUMFRIES on the first day of
the next Court to answer ELIAS EDMONDS and WALTER GRAHAM of a Plea of
Trespass on the Case damage seventy five pounds, and have then there this Writ.
Witness HUMPHREY BROOKE, Clerk of our Court at DUMFRIES the 29th day of
October in the 14th year of the Commonwealth A. D. 1789
                              H. BROOKE, C. D. D. C.
      For money due by Promissory Note
                              BUCHANAN for Plaintiff
      May 1790   Common Order
      August 1790   Continuance for Declaration
      November 1790   Same
      December 1790   Declaration filed, Common Order confirmed
                              & Inquiry
To wit. ELIAS EDMONDS, Assignee of WALTER GRAHAM, complains of
RICHARD S. BLACKBURN in custody &c. for that whereas the defendant on the
ninth day of January in the year one thousand seven hundred and eighty six at the
County aforesaid being indebted to WALTER GRAHAM made his Promissory Note
in writing subscribed with his proper hand and thereby promised and bound himself

his heirs &c. to pay to WALTER GRAHAM or his assigns the sum of sixty four pounds, fourteen shillings on or before the ninth day of January one thousand seven hundred and eighty seven and WALTER GRAHAM afterwards, viz., the twenty seventh day of September in the year last mentioned at the County aforesaid and before the sum of money was paid did assign over the Note to the Plaintiff by an endorsement in writing on the back thereof whereof the Defendant then and thre had notice, by reason of which and by force of the Act of Assembly in that case made, action accrued to the Plaintiff to demand and have of the Defendant the sum of sixty four pounds, fourteen shillings, yet the Defendant not regarding his promise but

p.   Edmonds v Blackburn
218   intending to deceive the Plaintiff in this behalf tho often required &c. hath not
         paid the sum of money to the Plaintiff but the same to pay hath refused and
still doth refuse to the Plaintiff's damage seventy five pounds, and therefore he brings suit, &c.

                                        BUCHANAN for Plaintiff

         Pledges &c. J. Doe & R. Roe
January 9th 1786
         I hereby bind myself my heirs Executors Administrators or assigns to pay to
Mr. WALTER GRAHAM or his assigns sixty four pounds, fourteen shillings on or before the ninth day of January 1787. Witness my hand
                         RICHARD S. BLACKBURN
         Eight Guineas of the above sum paid to me,
                         WALTER GRAHAM as also three pounds, ten shillings
         I hereby assign fifty pounds of the within Note to Colo. ELIAS EDMONDS [it being all due on the Note for value received of EDMONDS as witness my hand this 27th September 87
                         WALTER GRAHAM
October 16th 1793
         ELIAS EDMONDS, Assignee of WALTER GRAHAM, Plaintiff   ]
                 against   ] In Case
         RICHARD SCOTT BLACKBURN, Defendant   ]
This day came the parties by their Attornies and thereupon came a Jury to wit;

WILLIAM GUNYON	NATHANIEL TRIPLETT	SHADRACK RATCLIFFE
JOHN HEDGES	JOHN GIBSON	WILLIAM HULETT
WILLIAM BEALE	GEORGE WILLIAMS	THOMAS THORNTON
WILDMAN KINCHELOE	JOSEPH BRADY and	JOSEPH NELSON

who being elected tried and sworn the truth to speak upon the issue joined upon their Oath do say that the Defendant did assume upon himself in manner and form as by replying the Plaintiff hath alledged and they do assess the Plaintiff's damages by means thereof to sixty six pounds, eight shillings and four pence besides his costs; therefore it is considered by the Court that the Plaintiff recover against the Defendant his damages in form assessed and his costs by him about his suit in this behalf expended, and the Defendant in mercy, &c.

         Plaintiff's costs   115 lbs tobacco @ 1 1/2   ]
                                60 lbs tobacco @ 1 1/4   ] p pound & $9.72
         Execution issued

p.   Conn v West
219   The Commonwealth of Virginia to the Sheriff of FAIRFAX County, Greeting;
       You are hereby commanded to take THOMAS WEST if he be found within your
Bailiwick and him safely keep so that you have his body before the Judges of the
District Court to be holden at the Town of DUMFRIES on the first day of the next
Court to answer GERRARD TRAMMELL CONN of a Plea of Trespass, Assault and
Battery and False Imprisonment, damage one thousand pounds, And have then and
there this Writ. Witness HUMPHREY BROOKE, Clerk of our Court at DUMFRIES
the twenty seventh day of April A. D. 1789 and in the xiii year of the Commonwealth
                                    H. BROOKE, C. D. D. C.
       For False Imprisonment   SIMMS for Plaintiff
       Executed p BALDWIN DADE
FAIRFAX County to wit;
       GERRARD TRAMMELL CONN complains of THOMAS WEST in custody and
so forth for this that the Defendant on the [blank] day of [blank] in the year of our Lord
one thousand seven hundred and eighty nine at the Parish of Fairfax in the County
aforesaid with force and arms on him the Plaintiff an assault did make and him the
Plaintiff did then and there beat wound imprison and ill treat and him the Plaintiff
there in Prison without any reasonable cause and against the Law and custom of this
Commonwealth of Virginia a long time, to wit, for the space of sixty days from thence
next ensuing did detain untill the Plaintiff expended and laid out and was obliged and
compelled to expend and lay out several large sums of money for his deliverance from
the arrest and imprisonment and other outrages to the Plaintiff then and there did
against the peace and dignity of the Commonwealth whereby he says he is prejudiced
and hath damage to the value of 1000 pounds and therefore he brings suit, &c.
                                    SIMMS for Plaintiff

       Pledges &c. J. Doe & R. Roe
       May 1789   Common Order against Defendant
       July 1789   Common Order confirmed and Inquiry

p.   Conn v West
220   October 1793   Inquiry set aside and Not Guilty joined

       [The remainder of page 220 is blank, and all of pages 221, 222, 223 and 224 are blank.]

p.   Duncan v Lee
225   ANN DUNCAN, Plaintiff   ]
                against   ] In Case
       THOMAS LEE, Defendant   ]
       This suit is discontinued being agreed by the parties

       The Commonwealth of Virginia to the Sheriff of Prince William County,
Greeting. We command you that you take THOMAS LEE, SENR. if he be found
within your Bailiwick and him safely keep so that you have his body before the
Judges of the District Court to be held at the Town of DUMFRIES at the next Court

to answer ANN DUNCAN of a Plea of Trespass on the Case damage three hundred pounds; And have then there this Writ. Witness GEORGE BROOKE Clerk of the Court at DUMFRIES the 15th day of April in the 14th year of the Commonwealth A. D. 1790

G. BROOKE, C. D. D. C.

For money due by Account, no Bail required   MINOR
Executed   JAMES TRIPLETT, D Sh.

Prince William County, to wit

ANN DUNCAN complains of THOMAS LEE, SENR. in custody, &c. for this, to wit, that whereas the Defendant on the [blank] day of [blank] in the year of our Lord 178[blank] at PHILADELPHIA, that is to say, in the County of Prince William, was indebted to the Plaintiff in [blank] in divers goods wares and merchandizes before that time sold and delivered to the Defendant and for work and service done by the Plaintiff at the special instance and request of the Defendant, and being so indebted he, the Defendant, in consideration thereof afterwards, to wit, on the same day and year aforesaid at Prince William aforesaid undertook and then and there promised the Plaintiff to pay her the sum of whatever he should be thereunto required and whereas afterwards, to wit, on the same day and year aforesaid, at Prince William aforesaid, the Defendant in consideration that the Plaintiff had at the special instance and request of the Defendant sold and delivered to him divers other goods wares and merchandizes and performed other work and service undertook and then and there faithfully promised the Plaintiff that he would well and truly

p.   Duncan v Lee
226   pay and satisfy unto her as much money as she reasonbably deserved to
        have, therefore the Plaintiff avers tht she reasonably deserved to have for the
last mentioned goods and work other [blank] of which the Defendant then and there had notice, nevertheless the Defendant contriving and fraudulently intending to deceive and defraud the Plaintiff in this behalf hath not yet paid the sum of [blank] to her but hitherto to pay the same hath refused and still doth refuse to the damage of the Plaintiff [blank] pounds, therefore she brings suit &c.

JELLINOR for Plaintiff

June 1790	Special Imparlance and ruled to Security for costs
August 1790	Rule continued
November 1790	Rule to plead
February 1791	Continued Plea
March 1791	do
April 1791	Non Assumpsit joined

THOMAS LEE Esqr. Dr. to ANN DUNCAN

1793 Aug 19th   For goods per Account rendered. Had 6th October 1782   102.....0.....2 1/2
                  Interest from 1 January 1793 till this day is ten years
                  seven months & 1/2 @ 6 p cent pr annum   62...19...10
                                                                           165.....0.....0 1/2

PHILADELPHIA, August the 20th 1793. I have this day received from Mr. THOMAS LEE, SENR., one hundred fifty pounds current money of Virginia being in full for all demands agaisnt Mr. LEE to this date and for which a suit is now depending in the District Court of Virginia in the Prince William District; I also do hereby authorize THOMAS LEE, SENR. to have the aforementioned suit of mine against him dismised

Witness ROBERT HENRY DUNKIN   ANN DUNKIN

p.   Farrell v West
227   The Commonwealth of Virginia to the Sheriff of FAIRFAX County, Greeting;
We command you that you take ROGER WEST if he be found within your
Bailiwick and him safely keep so that you hve his body before the Judges of the
District Court to be held at the Town of DUMFRIES at the next Court to anwer
THOMAS FARRELL of a Plea of Trespass Assault and Battery, damage five hundred pounds, and have then there this Writ. Witness GEORGE BROOKE, Clerk of
the Court at DUMFRIES the 24th day of July in the 15th year of the Common-
wealth A. D. 1790

                   G. BROOKE, C. D. D. C.

    For Trespass Assault and Battery committed by the Defendant on the
Plaintiff   C. SIMMS for Plaintiff

    Executed pr BALDWIN DADE
FAIRFAX, to wit

    THOMAS FARRELL complains of ROGER WEST in custody &c. for this to
wit that the Defendant on the [blank] day of [blank] in the year of our Lord one thousand seven hundred and ninety at the Parish of Fairfax in the County aforesaid with
force and arms an assault did make on the Plaintiff and him, the Plaintiff, did beat,
wound and evil intreat and then and there did other wrongs and injuries to the Plaintiff
against the peace and dignity of the Commonwealth and to the damage of the Plaintiff [blank] pounds, whereupon he brings suit, &c.

                   SIMMS for the Plaintiff

Pledges &c. J. Doe & R. Roe
November 1790   Common Order
December 1790   Declaration filed, Common Order confirmed & Inquiry
October 16th 1793

     THOMAS FARRELL, Plaintiff   ]
           against   ]   In Trespass Assault and
     ROGER WEST, Defendant   ]   Battery
   This suit is discontinued, being agreed by the parties

p.   Davis v Howdyshell
228   The Commonwealth of Virginia to the Sheriff of LOUDOUN County, Greeting
    We command you that you take JACOB HOWDYSHELL if he be found within
your Bailiwick and him safely keep so that you have his body before the Judges of the
District Court to be held at the Town of DUMFRIES at the next Court to answer
RICHARD DAVIS by his next Friend, DAVID DAVIS, of a Plea of Trespass Assault
and Battery, damage two hundred pounds; and have then there this Writ. Witness
GEORGE BROOKE, Clerk of the Court at DUMFRIES the 13th day of August in the
15t year of the Commonwealth A. D. 1790

                   G. BROOKE, C. D. D. C.

For beating the Plaintiff
November 1790   Common Order
February 1791   Continued for Declaration
March 1791   Declaration filed
April 1791   Common Order confirmed and Inquiry

LOUDOUN County to wit
    RICHARD DAVIS complains of JACOB HOWDYSHELL in custody, &c. for
that whereas the Defendant on the [blank] day of [blank] in the year of our Lord one
thousand seven hundred and [blank] at the Parish of [blank] and County aforesaid
with force and arms did make an assault upon the Plaintiff and him then and there did
beat wound and evilly treat and then and there did other wrongs and injuries to the
Plaintiff against the peace of the Commonwealth and to the damage of the Plaintiff
two hundred pounds, and thereof he brings suit, &c.
                    HARRISON for Plaintiff

    Pledges &c. J. Doe & R. Roe

October 16th 1793
    RICHARD DAVIS, Plaintiff   ]
         against   ] In Trespass Assault and
    JACOB HOWDYSHELL, Defendant   ]   Battery
    This suit is discontinued, being agreed by the parties

p.   Coquit v Herbert
229   The Commonwealth of Virginia to the Sheriff of FAIRFAX County, Greeting
    We command you that you take WILLIAM HERBERT if he be found within
your Bailiwick and him safely keep so that you have his body before the Judges of the
District Court to be held at the Town of DUMFRIES at the next Court to answer
MARC ANTOINE COQUIT de FRAIZAILE of a Plea of Trespass Assault and false
imprisonment, damage one thousand pounds, and have then there this Writ. Witness
GEORGE BROOKE, Clerk of the Court at DUMFRIES this 3d day of September in
the 15th year of the Commonwealth A. D. 1790
                    G. BROOKE, C. D. D. C.
    For Trespass Assault and false imprisonment
    Executed pr BALDWIN DADE
FAIRFAX Courtny, to wit
    MARC ANTOINE COQUIT d FRAZAILE complains of WILLIAM HERBERT
in custody &c., for this to wit that whereas the Defendant on the [blank] day of [blank]
in the year one thousand seven hundred and ninety at the Parish of Fairfax and County aforesaid, with force and arms, to wit, with swords, staves and knives on him the
Plaintiff in the Parish and County aforesaid did make an assault and him, the Plaintiff did then and there beat wound imprison and ill treat and him, the Plaintiff, there in
Prison without any reasonable cause and against the Law and custom of this Com-
monweealth did detain untill the Plaintiff expended and laid out and was obliged and
compelled to expend and lay out several large sums of money for his deliverance from

arrest and imprisonment and other outrages on him the Plaintiff then and there committed against the peace and dignity of the Commonwealth and to the damage of him the Plaintiff one thousand pounds, therefore he brings his suit, &c.

SIMMS for Plaintiff

Pledges &c. J. Doe & R. Roe	
November 1790	Special Imparlance, Declaration filed
December 1790	Rule to plead

p.   Coquit v Herbert
230

January 1791	Continued Plea
February 1791	do
March 1791	do
April 1791	Judgment by default and Inquiry

To CHARLES SIMMS, Esqr., Attorney at Law

Sir. Please to take notice tht I require security for payment of the costs which may be awarded to me and also of the fees which will become due to the Officers of the Court in the suit now pending in the District Court holden at DUMFRIES in which COQUIT is Plaintiff and I am Defendant and that I require the aforesaid security to be given according to Law

25th July 1792

I am your Honorable Servant
WILLIAM HERBERT

FAIRFAX County to wit

Personally appeared CHARLES TURNER before me a Justice of the Peace for the County and made Oath that [blank] COQUIT was on the twenty first day of July in the year 1792 was not resident in the Commonwealth of Virginia as he believes and that he delvered to CHARLES SIMMS, Esqr. a practicing Attorney in the District Court held at DUMFRIES a writing whereof the above is a copy on thetwentieth day of August in the year 1792. Given under my hand this 20th day of August in the year 1792.

R. WEST

October 16, 1793

MARC ANTOINE QOQUETTE de FRAZAILE, Plaintiff	] In Trespass
against	] Assault and
WILLIAM HERBERT, Defendant	] Battery

This suit is discontinued being agreed by the parties

Lucas v McIntosh

The Commonwealth of Virginia to the Sheriff of LOUDOUN County, Greeting; We command you that you take LOY McINTOSH if he be found within your Bailiwick and him safely keep so that you have his body before the Judges of the District Court to be held at the Town of DUMFRIES at the next Court to answer ROBERT LUCAS of a Plea of Trespass Assault and Battery, damage five hundred pounds, And have then there this Writ. Witness GEORGE BROOKE, Clerk of our Court at DUMFRIES the 26th day of April in the 14th year of the Commonwealth A. D. 1790

G. BROOKE, C. D. D. C.

p.   Lucas v McIntosh
231   For Assault and Battery

                                        SIMMS for the Plaintiff

        June 1790   Common Order
        August 1790   Continued, Declaration
LOUDOUN to wit
        ROBERT LUCAS complains of LOY McINTOSH in custody, &c., for this, to
wit, that the Defendant on the [blank] day of [blank] in the year of our Lord [blank] at
the Parish of [blank] in the County aforesaid with force and arms an assault did make
on the Plaintiff and him, the Plaintiff, did beat wound and eveil intreat and then and
there did other wrongs and injuries to the Plaintiff againt the peace and dignity of the
Commonwealth and to the damage of the Plaintiff [blank] pounds, and thereupon he
brings suit, &c.

                                        SIMMS for the Plaintiff

        Pledges &c. J. Doe & R. Roe
        November 1790   Continued for Declaration
        December 1790   Common Order confirmed and Inquiry
        This suit abates by the death of the Plaintiff

        Muir v Terrett
        The Commonwealth of Virginia to the Sheriff of FAIRFAX County Greeting.
We command you that you take WILLIAM HENRY TERRETT if he be found within
your Bailiwick and him safely keep so that you have his body before the Judges of the
District Court to be held at the Town of DUMFRIES at the next Court to answer
JOHN MUIR of a Plea of Trespass on the Case, damage one hundred pounds, And
have then there this Writ. Witness GEORGE BROOKE, Clerk of the Court at DUM-
FRIES this 28th day of September in the 15th year of the Commonwealth A. D. 1790
                                        G. BROOKE C. D.. D. C.

        For money due by Account
        Executed CHARLES TURNER, S S

p.   Muir v Terrett
232   FAIRFAX County to wit
        JOHN MUIR complains of WILLIAM HENRY TERRETT in custody, &c., for
that whereas the Defendant on the 17th day of February 1787 at the Parish of Fairfax and County aforesaid was indebted unto the Plaintiff the sum of fifty eight pounds
nine shillings and an half penny current money of Virginia for divers goods wares and
merchandizes by the Plaintiff to the same Defendant at his special instance and request before that time has sold and deliverd and so being therein indebted, the Defendant in consideration thereof afterwards, to wit, the same day and year at the Parish
and County aforesaid assumed upon himself and to the Plaintiff then and there faithfully promised to pay him that sum, and whereas the same Defendant afterwards, to
wit, the day and year aforesaid in the Parish and County aforesaid, in consideration
that the Plaintiff at the like special instance and request of the Defendant before that
time had there sold and delivered to the same Defendant other goods wares and mer-

chandizes assumed upon himself and to the Plaintiff then and there faithfully promised to pay him so much money as the last mentioned goods wares and merchandizes were reasonably worth and the Plaintiff in fact says that the last mentioned
goods wares and merchandizes were reasonably worth other fifty eight pounds, nine
shillings and an half penny like current money of Virginia whereof the Defendant the
day year and place last mentioned had notice; Nevertheless the Defendant his several
promises and assumptions in form made not regarding but contriving and fraudulently intending the Plainttif in this behalf craftily and subtlely to deceive and defraud the
several sums of money or any penny thereof to the Plaintiff [altho thereto often
afterwards required] hath not yet paid but the same to him to pay hath hitherto altogether refused and still doth refuse to the damage of the Plaintiff [blank] pounds,
therefore he brings suit, &c.

SIMMS for the Plaintiff

Pledges &c. J. Doe & R. Roe
November 1790   Declaration filed, Common Order
December 1790   Bail filed, Common Order set aside and Special
                                        Imparlance
January 1791   Rule to plead
February & March 1791 Continued for Plea
April 1791   Judgment by Defendant and Inquiry

p.   Muir v Terrett
233   Memorandum: That upon the eighth day of October in the year 1790, JOHN
       C. HUNTER of the County of FAIRFAX personally appeared before me,
WILLIAM HERBERT, Gentleman, one of the persons appointed by the General
Court for taking Special Bail within the County of FAIRFAX and undertook for
WILLIAM HENRY TERRETT at the suit of JOHN MUIR in an action of Debt now
depending in the District Court of DUMFRIES that in case WILLIAM HENRY
TERRETT shall be cast in the suit he, WILLIAM HENRY TERRETT, will pay and
satisfy the condemnation of the Court or render his body to Prison in Execution for
the same or that he, JOHN CHAPMAN HUNTER, will do it for him;

W. HERBERT

Dr. Mr. WILLIAM HENRY TERRETT,   Sterling   Currency
     To JOHN MUIR

1762			Sterling	Currency
October 16	To 4 3/4 yards Bath Coating @ 4/ is 19/ and 4 yards ditto at 3/9 is 15/		1...14.....0	
	To 14 yards binding 1/2 & 5 1/4 yards London Quality 8d.		1...10	
	To 4 1/2 yards 4/4 Shaloon @ 1/3 is 5/3 3/4 and 1/2 yard Buckram at 5d		5.....8 3/4	
	To 4 hank large sewing silk 2/8; & 2 ounces thread 5d		1.....1	
	To 2 yards green holland 2/ & 3 1/4 doz Basket Oats 2/2		4.....2	
	To 2 small Vests 1d., 3/4 yards green Linen 6d, 1 yard flannell @ 1/2		1.....9	
24	To 1 1/2 yards bath coating		6.....0	
November 8	To 1 m 10d Nails 4/10 1/2; 4m 8d ditto 2/9 1/2; and 150 20d ditto 1/		9.....8	
December 3	To 1 Crupper 6d., 1 claw hammer 11d., 1 1/2 yards black Ribbon		1...11	
15	To Cash 102/ and 1 pin knife 1/			5.....3

[The Account William Henry Terrett to John Muir continues for four and an half more pages for purchases made
December 22, 1762.   February 19, 1763, March 3, 1763, April 12, 26 and 27, 1763.

p.   Muir v Terrett
234   Account William Henry Terrett to John Muir continued all this page half of which appears to be for some year through December, then purchases made in 1774 from January 17 through May 6.

p.   Muir v Terrett
235   Account of William Henry Terrett to John Muir continued all this page for purchases made from June 1774 through November 1774.. An entry for September 15, 1774 "To one pair mens shoes 9/, 1 yard linen for W. MUN-ROE," September 29, 1774, "To one pair men's shoes for W. MONROE", November 12, 1774 "To 7 yards fine Linen for W. MUNROE
At the end of 1774, the Account Debit was 44.....4.....1 1/2 in Sterling and 45...16...7 1/2 in currency. On February 18, 1775, an entry "to the balance of Miss NANCY's silk hat."

p.   Muir v Terrett
236   Account of William Henry Terrett to John Muir continues for purchases made from April 10, 1775 through December 27, 1775. The June 13, 1775 entry "To Mr. RICHARD SANDFORD, Inspector, 275."; October 2, 1775. "To Mr. JOHN LUKE for a 1/2 yard persian", Balance at end of 1775: 23....2.....0 1/2 sterling; 34.....2.....9 1/2 currency.

p.   Muir v Territt
237   Account of William Henry Terret to John Muir continues for purchasdes made in 1775, An account balance on February 17, 1787; In 1772, 1773, 1774, 1775 and 1781 there are a number of entries for cirdit for Wheat, for the HUNTING CREEK Crop, also sold Wood at various times

p.   Muir v Terrett
238   FAIRFAX County, to wit
        JOHN MUIR personally appeared before me the Subscriber, one of the Magistrates for the County and made Oath on the Holy Evangelists that the fore-going Account is just and true and that he hath received no part thereof or satisfaction for the same other than is credited; Given under my hand this 24th day of September 1790

                                    JOHN POTTS, JUNR.

Dr. Mr. WILLIAM HENRY TERRETT   To JOHN MUIR
1774 Feb.   To Interest on L. 32.....6..10 for ten years till February 1784   16.....2.....6
              To Interest on L. 35 from February 1774 till February 1784
                 running Account say five years   8...15.....0
1784 Feb.   To Interest on L. 58.....9 till February 1787 being 3 years   8...14...11
                                                                                       33...11.....6

1781 Mr. JOHN MUIR to WILLIAM HENRY TERRETT DR
1784 To 15 cords of Wood   15.....0.....0

Sir. I received yours and I am sorry it has not been in my power to settle with you before this, owing entirely to disappointments from those who are indebted to me mor than I owe. I am about prising my tobacco and as soon as I can get it to the Warehouse and inspected, I will let you have it. I am Sir, your Obedient Servant

W. HY. TERRETT

June 9th 1786

PS I should be glad you would send me the amount of my Account.

Yrs. W. T.

Mr. JOHN MUIR.

Sir. I received your Letter by Mr. BOWIE. Am sorry it has never been in my power to pay you off the Account that stands against me, the tobacco I told you I had my Overseer packed away in the Fodder House and let the Hogs get at it and destroy it in such a manner that I am afraid there is a great deal washed; the winter has been so dry it has not been in my power to get what there is left in order to prize. I will call on you in a very short time and have the Account settled

I am your humble Servant

W. HY TERRETT to Mr. JOHN MUIR.

p. 239

Muir v Terrett

October 16, 1793.

JOHN MUIR, Plaintiff   ]
against   ] In Case
WILLIAM HENRY TERRETT, Defendant]

This suit abates by the death of the Plaintiff

Duffy v Summers

The Commonwealth of Virginia to the Sheriff of FAIRFAX County, Greeting. We command you that you take WILLIAM SUMMERS if he be found within your Bailiwick and him safely keep so that you have his body before the Judges of the District Court to be held at the Town of DUMFRIES on the first day of the next Court to answer BARTHOLOMEW DUFFY of a Plea of Trespass on the Case, damage five hundred pounds, And have then there this Writ. Witness HUMPHREY BROOKE, Clerk of the Court at DUMFRIES the fourth day of August in the fourteenth year of the Commonwealth A. D. 1789

H. BROOKE, C. D. D. C.

An action for illegal imprisonment

J. LOVE for Plaintiff

Executed   pr BALDWIN DADE

October 1789	Special Imparlance
January 1790	Rule to plead
March 1790	Not Guilty and Justification and time to reply
April 1790	Continued, Replication
February 1791	Same
March 1791	do.
April 1791	Joinder & Issue Not Guilty set aside by consent

FAIRFAX County, to wit

BARTHOLOMEW DUFFY complains of WILLIAM SUMMERS in custody and so forth of a Plea for this that WILLIAM SUMMERS on the [blank] day of [blank] in the year 1789 with force and arms, to wit, with swords, sticks and clubs upon the Plaintiff at the Parish of Fairfax in the County of FAIRFAX made an assault and him did beat wound and imprison and evilly treat as that of his life it was greatly despaired and also without any reasonable cause against the Laws of the Commonwealth and against the peace thereof then and there did unlawfully imprison

p.   Duffy v Summers
240   BARTHOLOMEW DUFFY and for a long time, that is to say, for the space of
           two days detained him in Prison and other wrongs to him then and there did to
the great damage of the Plaintiff and against the peace of the Commonwealth where-by the Plaintiff saith that he is damaged to the value of 500 pounds, and therefore he brings suit, &c.

                              CHARLES LEE for Plaintiff
           Pledges of prosecution, J. Doe & R. Roe

           The Commonwalth to the Sergeant of the COURT of HUSTINGS in the Town of ALEXANDRIA Greeting; You are hereby commanded to take BARTOLOMEW DUFFY if he be found within your Bailiwick and him safely keep so that you have his body before the Justices of the COURT of HUSTINGS in the Town of ALEXANDRIA on the Thursday after the third Monday in March next to answer JAMES CAMP-BELL of a Plea of Trespass on the Case damage two hundred pounds and have then and there this Writ; Witness PETER WAGENER, Clerk of the Court this 15th day of January 1789

                              P. WAGENER
           Endorsed. Executed and in custody, released by PATRICK MURRAY's be-coming Bail for appearance

                              WM. SUMMERS
TOWN of ALEXANDRIA, to wit

           JAMES CAMPBELL complains of BARTHOLOMEW DUFFY in custody and so forth for this, to wit, that whereas JAMES CAMPBELL the Plaintiff on the fif-teenth day of January in the year 1789 at the Parish of Fairfax and Town of ALEXANDRIA afterwards was a good faithful and honest citizen of the Common-wealth of Virginia and for a long space of time, viz. from the time of his birth to the time of speaking the false slanderous words hereafter mentioned hath been a good name and honest and fair reputation and hath so behaved himself in every place and more especially in the Town of ALEXANDRIA as to acquire the good opinion and con-fidence of all persons who were acquainted with him and more especially of such as resided in

p.   Duffy v Summers
241   the Town of ALEXANDRIA and by reason of his good name had obtained the
           lover and good will of all the people in the Town and others elsewhere and
whereas the Plaintiff now exerciseth and for a great space of time hath exercised the Trade of a Shoemaker and thereby and by reason of his good name and reputation

therein hath for many years got and endeavoured to get his livelihood in support of himself and family, Nevertheless BARTHOLOMEW DUFFY, the Defendant, being also an Inhabitant of the Town of ALEXANDRIA as well as the Plaintiff and both being within the jurisdiction of the COURT of HUSTINGS of the Town well knowing the premises but contriving and maliciously and wickedly intending to deprive him, the Plaintiff, of his good name fame credit and reputation and to bring him into scandal and reproach as well amongst all good persons as others and more especially amongst his good acquaintances and customers in the Town in certain discourse then and there, to wit, on the first day of January in the year 1789 at the Parish of Fairfax and within the Town of ALEXANDRIA within the jurisdiction of the COURT of HUSTINGS did falsely and maliciously in the hearing of many good citizens of the Commonwealth speak utter and with a loud voice proclaim of and concerning the Plaintiff the false slanderous and defamatory words following, to wit, "You [meaning the Plaintiff] are a little convicted fellow." thereby meaning the Plaintiff had been lawfully convicted of some offence punishable by Law and of an infamous nature and also there other words "You [meaning the Plaintiff] are a convicted puppy and I [himself the Defendant meaning] can prove it." thereby meaning to say that the Plaintiff had been legally convicted of some infamous or other crime punishable by Law by reason of which speaking of the several false scandalous and slanderous and defamatory words the Plaintiff is greatly injured in his good name and is greatly hurt in his Trade and business in so much that divers of his former Customers have refused to employ him therein or to deal with him

p.   <u>Duffy v Summers</u>
242   and the Plaintiff is much damaged in his Trade to his damage two hundred pounds and thereof he bring suit, &c.

CHARLES LEE for Plaintiff

Pledges of prosecution, J. Doe & R. Roe

1789 March Court	Special Imparlance
April	Rule narration
1789 May Court	Continued
June	Rule narration
July	Narration filed and time
August	Not Guilty joined

1790 March Court

JAMES CAMPBELL, Plaintiff	]	
against	]	Trespass on the Case
BARTHOMOMEW DUFFY, Defendant]		

This day came the parties by their Attornies and thereupon came a Jury, to wit

LEWIS WESTON	ANDREW WALES	ROBERT LYLE
GEORGE DARLING	JOHN WISE	JOHN SULLIVAN
BEAL HOWARD	ADAM FOIGER	WILLIAM WRIGHT
ROBERT COUPAR	ARCHIBALD McCLISH and	JOHN GRAHAM

the truth of the premises being elected tried and sworn upon their Oath do say that the Defendant the day year and place in the Declaration mentioned did speak and publish certain false slanderous and defamatory words of and concerning the Plaintiff in manner and form as the Plaintiff againnst him hath declared and assess the damages of the Plaintiff by reason of the speaking and publishing the slanderous and defamatory words in the Declaration mentioned to one penny; therefore it is considered that the Plaintiff recover against the Defendant the one penny damages by the Jurors in form assessed and the Defendant in mercy, &c.

ALEXANDRIA Sst
    I PETER WAGENER, Clerk of the Court of Hustings in the Town of ALEXANDRIA do hereby certify that the above and foregoing transcript of Record is a true copy from the Records of the Court in a suit wherein JAMES CAMPBELL is Plaintiff and BARTHOLOMEW

p.   Duffy v Summers
243   DUFFY is Defendant. In Testimony whereof I have hereunto set my hand this 10th day of May 1793
                            P. WAGENER, Cl Cur

October 16, 1793
    BARTHOMOMEW DUFFY, Plaintiff   ]
            against   ]   In Case
    WILLIAM SUMMERS, Defendant   ]
This day came the parties by their Attornies and thereupon came a Jury, to wit

PHILIP DAW	ALEXANDER KEITH	THOMAS BLINCOE
ALEXANDER LITHGOW	WILLIAM LAWSON	JAMES MOTHERWELL
WILLIAM SMITH	JESSE TAYLOR	THOMAS JAMES
MUNGO HANCOCK	JOHN MORRISON and	JOHN LAWSON

who being elected tried and sworn the truth to speak upon the issue joined upon their Oath do say that the Defendant is Not Guulty in manner and form as Plaitiff by replying hath alledged; therefore it is considered by the Court that Plaintiff take nothing by his Bill but for his false clamour be in mercy, &c., and that the Defendant go thereof without day and recover against the Plaintiff his costs by him about his defence in this behalf expended

Bennett v Herbert
    The Commonweath of Virginia to the Sheriff of FAIRFAX County Greeting; We command you that you take THOMAS HERBERT if he be found in your Bailiwick and him safely keep so as to have his body before the Judges of the District Court to be held at the Town of DUMFRIES at the next Court to answer HENRY ASTLEY BENNETT, Esquire, of a Plea of Debt for thirty eight pounds, six shillings current money, damage ten pounds, and have then there this Writ. Witness GEORGE BROOKE, Clerk of the Court at DUMFRIES the 17th day of September in the 15th year of the Commonwealth A. D. 1790
                            G. BROOKE, C. D. D. C.
    For Debt due on Bond, Bail is required
                            CHARLES SIMMS for Plaintiff
    Executed BENJAMIN FAIRFAX Bail
                    pr   BALDWIN DADE
    KNOW ALL MEN by these presents that we THOMAS HERBERT and BENJAMIN FAIRFAX are held and firmly bound unto ROBERT TOWNSHEND

HOOE,

p.   Bennett v Herbert
244   Sheriff of FAIRFAX County in the just and full sum of seventy six pounds,
        twelve shillings current money of Virginia to be paid unto ROBERT T. HOOE
his Executors Administrators or assigns to which payment well and truly to be made
we bind ourselves and each of us our and each of our heirs Executors and Administrators jointly and severally firmly by these presents; Sealed with our seals and dated
this 9th day of October 1790
        Whereas HENRY ASTLEY BENNETT hath sued forth agaisnt THOMAS
HERBERT out of the District Court of DUMFRIES a Writ of capias ad respondendum in a Plea of Debt for thirty eight pounds, six shillings, damage ten pounds
directed unto the Sheriff of FAIRFAX County which hath been executed upon
THOMAS HERBERT;
        Now the Condition of the above Obligation is such that if the above bound
THOMAS HERBERT do make his personal appearance at the next Court to be held
for the District at the Courthouse at DUMFRIES on the first day of October Court
and do then and there abide by, perform and fulfill such orders as by the Court shall
be made in the action and do not depart from the Court till the same shall be performed, then the above obligation to be void, or else to remain in full force power and
virtue in Law
Signed and delivered in presence of
        B. DADE   THOMAS HERBERT   [seal]
                                             BENJAMIN FAIRFAX [seal]
FAIRFAX County, to wit
        HENRY ASTLEY BENNETT, Esqr. complains of THOMAS HERBERT in
custody, &c. of a Plea that he render unto him the just and full sum of thirty eight
pounds, six shillings currency which to him he owes and from him unjustly detains for
that whereas the Defendant on the 5th day of January in the year of our Lord 1789,
at the Parish of Fairfax and County aforesaid did by his certain Writing Obligatory
sealed with his seal and to the Court now here shewn the date is the same day and
year, acknowledged himself to be held and firmly bound to the Plaintiff in the sum of
thirty eight pounds, six shillings currency to be paid to the Plaintiff when

p.   Bennett v Herbert
245   the Defendant should be thereunto afterwards required yet the Defendant
        altho thereto often required the sum of money or any penny thereof to the
Plaintiff hath not paid but the same to him to pay hath hitherto altogether refused
and still doth refuse to the damage of the Plaintiff [blank] pounds, therefore he brings
suit, &c.
                        SIMMS for the Plaintiff
Pledges of prosecution; J. Doe v R. Roe
        November 1790   Common Order against Defendant and Security
        Dece,ber 1790   Declaration filed, Common Order confirmed
        May 1791   Common Order set aside and payment for security
        KNOW ALL MEN by these presents that we THOMAS HERBERT and [blank]
of the County of FAIRFAX in Virginia are held and firmly bound unto HENRY

ASTLEY BENNETT, Esqr., of the Kingdom of Great Britain in the full and just sum of thirty eight pounds, six shillings currency to be paid to HENRY ASTLEY BENNETT Esqr. his certain Attorney Executors Administrators or assigns to the which payment well and truly to be made and done we bind ourselves our heirs Executors and Administrators jointly and severally firmly by these presents; Sealed with our seals and dated this 5th day of January in the year of our Lord one thousand seven hundred and eighty nine

THE CONDITION of the above Obligation is such that if the above bound THOMAS HERBERT do and shall well and truly pay or cause to be paid unto HENRY ASTLEY BENNETT Esqr., his heirs Executors Administrators or assigns the full and just sum of nineteen pounds, three shillngs at or upon the fifth day of July next with lawful Interest from this day if not then paid then the above Obligation to be void or else to remain in full force and virtue in Law

Sealed and delivered in presence of
    R. HARRISON   THOMAS HERBERT   [seal]
    JOSEPH LEWIS

p.   Bennett v Herbert
246   HENRY ASTLEY BENNETT, Plaintiff   ]
          against   ] In Debt
    THOMAS HERBERT, Defendant   ]

This day came the parties by their Attornies and the Defendant relinquishing his former Plea acknowledged the Plaintiff's action against him; therefore it is considered by the Court that the Plaintiff recover against the Defendant and BENJAMIN FAIRFAX, his Security, thirty eight pounds, six shilllings currency, the Debt in the Declaration mentioned, and his costs by him about his suit in this behalf expended, and the Defendant in mercy, &c., But this Judgment may be discharged by the payment of nineteen pounds, three shillings with Interest thereon to be computed after the rate of five per centum per annum from the fifth day of January 1789 untill paid and the costs

    Plaintiff's costs   100 lbs tobacco @ 1 1/3]
                    60 lbs tobacco @ 1 1/4] p pounds & $7.54.

    Cooke v Adam's Admrs.
The Commonwealth of Virginia to the Sheriff of FAIRFAX County, Greeting. We command you take WILLIAM WILLSON, WILLIAM HERBERT, ROGER WEST and WILLIAM HUNTER, JUNR., Administrators with the Will annexed of ROBERT ADAM, deceased if they be found within his Bailiwick so that you have them before the Judges of the District Court to be held at the Town of DUMFRIES at the next Court to answer JOHN COOKE, Assignee of GEORGE MASON, of a Plea of Debt for four hundred twenty four pounds, nine shillings and two pence sterling money of Great Britain, damage five pounds, And have then there this Writ. Witness GEORGE BROOKE, Clerk of the Court at DUMFRIES this 26th day of April in the 14th year of the Commonwealth A. D. 1790

                           G. BROOKE, C. D. D. C.

Debt due on Bond. BRENT.
Executed pr BALDWIN DADE
June 1790   Common Order
August 1790   Continued for Declaration
FAIRFAX County, to wit
    JOHN COOKE, Assignee of GEORGE MASON

p.   Cooke v Adam's Admrx.
247   complains of WILLIAM WILLSON, WILLIAM HERBERT, ROGER WEST
       and WILLIAM HUNTER, JUNR., Administrators with the Will annexed of
ROBERT ADAM, deceased, in custody, &c. of a Plea that they render unto him the
sum of four hundred twenty four pounds, nine shillngs and two pence sterling money
of Great Britain which from him they unjustly detain for that, to wit, that whereas
ROBERT ADAM in his life time by his certain Writing Obligatory sealed with his seal
and to the Court now shewn, and dated the 19th day of June in PRINCE GEORGE
County in the State of MARYLAND acknowledged himself indebted to GEORGE
MASON in the sum of four hundred twenty four pounds, nine shillings and two pence
sterling money of Great Britain, and for the payment thereof to GEORGE MASON
his heirs Executors Administrators of assigns ROBERT ADAM bound himself his
heirs Executors and Administrators which Writing Obligatory being due and unpaid in
the year of our Lord 1785, by his certain Indorsement on the back thereof made
signed with his proper name of GEORGE MASON, by GEORGE himself in his own
handwriting and sealed with his seal assigned and transfered over to the Plaintiff of
wich Assignemtn ROBERT in his life time, to wit, on the 29th day of September had
notice, Nevertheless ROBERT in his life time though often thereto reqired by the
Plaintiff di dnot pay nor have the Deefendants though often required the sum of four
hundred twenty four pounds, nine shillings and two pence sterling money of Great
Britain or any part thereof wherefore the Plaintiff sasy is injured and hath damage to
the value of five pounds and therefore brings suit, &c.
                              RICHARD BRENT for Plaintiff
       Pledges of prosection, J Doe v R Roe
       November 1790   Continued for Declaration
       December 1790   Common Order confirmed
       May 1791   Common Order set aside and payment

p.   Cooke v Adam's Admrs.
248   KNOW ALL MEN by these presents that I ROBERT ADAM of the Town of
       ALEXANDRIA in the County of FAIRFAX and Colony of Virginia am held and
firmly bound unto GEORGE MASON of the same County and Colony in the just and
full sum of four hundred twenty four pounds, nine shillings and two pence sterling
money of Great Britain to be paid to GEORGE MASON his Executors Administrators and assigns or to his or their certain Attorney, to the which payment well and
truly to be made I bind myself my heirs Executors and Administrators firmly by
these presents; signed and sealed with my seal in PRINCE GEORGE County in the
Province of MARYLAND this 19th day of June and in the year of our Lord one thousand seven hundred and seventy
    THE CONDITION of the above obligation is such that if the above bound

ROBERT ADAM his heirs Executors or Administrators shall well and truly pay or
cause to be paid unto the above named GEORGE MASON his Executors Administrators or assigns or to his or their certain Attorney on or before the first day of May
next ensuing the date hereof the just and full sum of two hundred twelve pounds, four
shillings and seven pence sterling money of Great Britain together with six pounds for
every hundred pounds and so pro rate being the legal Interest within the Province of
MARYLAND p annum to be computed from the first day of May last past, then the
above obligation to be void otherwise to remain in full force and power
Signed sealed and delivered in the presence of us in
PRINCE GEORGE County in the Province of
MARYLAND   MATTHEW CAMPBELL   ROBERT ADAM   [seal]
        JAMES ADAM
        Received the Interest on the within Bond up t the first of May 1774 in settle-
ment of Accounts with Mr. ROBERT ADAM
                        pr G. MASON
        Received of Mr. ROBERT ADAM the Interest due on the within Bond up to the
1st day of May in the year 1785
                        pr G. MASON
        Received of Mr. ROBERT ADAM the Interest due on the within Bond up to the
1st day of May in the year 1786
                        JOHN COOKE

p.   Cooke v Adam's Admrs.
249   Received of Mr. ROBERT ADAM the Interest due on the above Bond up to
        the 1st day of May in the year 1787
                        JOHN COOKE
CHARLES County, Sct.
        September 29th 1785. GEORGE MASON made Oath on the Holy Evangelists
of Almighty God that he has received no part parcel security or satisfaction for the
within Bond except the above Credits
                        Sworn before JOHN DENT.
Charles County, Sct.
        I hereby assign transfer and make over all my right title interest and claim of
in and to the within Bond to Colo. JOHN COOK of STAFFORD County in the Commonwealth of Virginia for value received; Witness my hand and seal this 29th day of
September 1785
Test JOHN DENT.   G. MASON   [seal]

October 16th 1793
        JOHN COOKE, Assignee of GEORGE MASON, Plaintiff   ]
                against   ]   In Debt
        WILLIAM WILLSON, WILLIAM HERBERT, ROGER   ]
        WEST and WILLIAM HUNTER, JUNR. Administrators   ]
        with the Will annexed of ROBERT ADAM, deceased,   ]
        Defendants   ]
     This day came the parties by their Attornies and this suit abates as to the Defen-
dant, HUNTER, by his death, and the Surviving Defendants relinquishing their for-

mer Plea acknowledged the Plaintiff's action agaisnt them; therefore it is considered by the Court that the Plaintiff recover against the Defendants four hundred twenty four pounds, nine shillings and two pence sterling money of Great Britain, the Debt in the Declaration mentioned, and his costs by him about his suit in this behalf expended to be levied of the goods and chatles of the deceased at the time of his death in the hands of the Defendants to be administered if so much thereof in their hands they have but if not then the costs to be levied of their own proper goods and chattles and the Defendants in mercy, &c., But this Judgment may be discharged by the payment of two hundred twelve pounds, four shillings and seven pence sterling money of Great Britain with Interest thereon to be computed after the rate of six per centum per annum from the first day of May 1787 untill paid and the costs

p.   Fairfax's Exrs. v Craig [or Craik]
250   The Commonwealth of Virginia to the Sheriff of FAIRFAX County, Greeting.
    We command you that you take JAMES CRAIG if he be found within your Bailiwick and him safely keep so that you have his body before the Judges of the District Court to be held at the Town of DUMFRIES at the next Court to answer GABRIEL JONES and THOMAS BRYAN MARTIN, Surviving Executors of the Last Will and Testament of the Right Honorable THOMAS LORD FAIRFAX, deceased, of a Plea of Debt for one hundred pounds, damage three hundred pounds, and have then there this Writ. Witness GEORGE BROOKE, Clerk of the Court at DUMFRIES the 21st day of September in the 15th year of the Commonwealth A.D. 1790
                    G. BROOKE, C. D. C.
    On Bond for payment of money.
                    C. LEE, p Plaintiff
    Executed, JAMES CRAIG, JUNR. Appearance Bail
                CHARLES TURNER, S. S.
    KNOW ALL MEN by these presents that we JAMES CRAIK and [blank] of County of FAIRFAX are held and firmly bound unto ROBERT TOWNSHEND HOOE Sheriff of FAIRFAX County in the full and just sum of two hundred pounds current money of Virginia to be paid unto ROBERT T. HOOE his Executors Administrators or assigns, to which payment well and truly to be made we bind ourselves and each of us our heirs Executors and Administrators jointly and severally firmly by these presents; Sealed with our seals and dated this 16th day of October 1790
    Whereas GABRIEL JONES and THOMAS BRYAN MARTIN, Surviving Executors of the Last Will and Testament of the Right Honorable THOMAS LORD FAIRFAX deceased, hath sued forth against JAMES CRAIK out of the District Court of DUMFRIES a Writ of capias ad respondendum in a Plea of Debt for one hundred pounds, damage three hundred pounds, directed to the Sheriff of the County of FAIRFAX which hath been executed upon JAMES CRAIK.
    Now the Condition of the above Obligation is such that if the above bound JAMES CRAIK do make his personal appearance at the next Court to be held for the District at the Courthouse in DUMFRIES on the first day of the Court and do then and there abide by, fulfill and perlform such orders by the Court shall be made in the action and not depart from the Court till the same shall be performed then

p.   Fairfax's Exrs. v Craig [or Craik]
251   the above Obligation to be void or else to remain in full force power and virtue
        in Law
Signed and delivered in presence of
        CHARLES TURNER   JAMES CRAIK   [seal]
                                                 JAMES CRAIK, JUNR. [seal]

FAIRFAX County, to wit
        GABRIEL JONES and THOMAS BRYAN MARTIN, Surviving Executors of
the Last Will and Testament of the Right Honorable THOMAS LORD FAIRFAX, the
other Executor of the Will being dead, complain of JAMES CRAIK in custody and so
forth of a Plea that he rended to them the sum of one hundred pounds current money
of Virginia with Interest from the fourth day of May in the year 1762 which from
them he detains for this, to wit, that whereas the Deendant on the 4th day of May in
the year 1762 at the Parish of [blank] in the County aforesaid, made his certain Note
in writing signed with his name and hand which is here shewn to the Court, the date
whereof is on the same day and year aforesaid and thereby promised to pay to THO-
MAS LORD FAIRFAX, his Executors Administrators or assigns the sum of one hundred pounds current money of Virginia with Interest from the date of the Note, Nevertheless the Defenant though often required hath not paid to THOMAS LORD FAIR-
FAX in his life time nor to any of his Execuors since his death the sum of money but
hath hitherto refused and still doth refuse to pay the same to the Plaintiffs to their
damage three hundred pounds and therefore and by force of the Act of Assembly in
such case made the sue &c., and they bring into Court Letters Testamentary whereby it appears they are Executors of the Last Will and Testament &c.
                                        CHARLES LEE for Plaintiffs

        Pledges of prosecution, J. Doe & R. Roe
        November 1790   Common Order against Defendant and Security
        December 1790   Declaration filed, Common Order confirmed
        May 1791   Common Order set aside and payment by Security

p.   Fairfax's Exrs. v Craig
252   I promise to pay to the Right Honorable THOMAS LORD FAIRFAX his Exe-
        cutors Administrators or assigns the sum of one hundred pounds current
money of Virginia with Interest from the date hereof for value received; Witness my
hand this fourth day of May 1762
                                        JAMES CRAIK

        Dear Sir:
        I received Mr. GELDART's Letter on the subject of the debt due to the Estate
of FAIRFAX and am extremely sorry that you should have been under the necessity
of making another application for the money. I left WINCHESTER and thought I
have taken the necessary steps to have the debt immediately discharged by money
received by Mr. KEITH on my Account. In this I was disappointed. The money has
been left in Mr. KEITH's hands to this day for the above purpose. Immediately on
the receipt of Mr. GELDART's Letter I called on that Gentleman who informed me he
would take immediate steps to have it settled and he has since told me that he has
wrote to you on the subject. I am much obliged by politeness and friendship in giving
me notice of the necessity of bringing suits for the debts due the Estate, and I flatter

myself Mr. KEITH will take the necessary steps to prevent it in my case, Should however this Gentleman deceive me, you may depend upon my taking the most ready steps in my power to satisfy the claim, I am Sir

ALEXANDRIA
    October 1st 1789

with respect
Your most obedient servant
    JAMES CRAIK

THOMAS BRYAN MARTIN, Greenway Court

October 16th 1793

GABRIEL JONES & THOMAS BRYAN MARTIN, Surviving]
Executors of the Last Will and Testament of the Right Honorable]
THOMAS LORD FAIRFAX, deceased, Plaintiffs]
        against] In Debt
JAMES CRAIK]

    This day came the parties by their Attornies and thereupon came also a Jury to wit

WILLIAM GUNYON	NATHANIEL TRIPLETT	SHADRACK RATCLIFF
JOHN HEDGES	JOHN GIBSON	WILLIAM HULETT
WILLIAM BEALE		

p. 253   <u>Fairfax's Exrs. v Craig [or Craik]</u>

	GEORGE WILLIAMS	THOMAS THORNTON
WILDMAN KINCHELOE	JOSEPH BRADY and	JOSEPH NELSON

who being elected tried and sworn the truth to speak upon the issue joined upon their Oath do say that the Defendant hath not paid the Debt in the Declaration mentioned as by replying the Plaintiffs have alledged and they do assess the Plaintiffs's damages by reason of the detention of that debt to one hundred and fifty seven pounds, one shillings and eight pence besides their costs; therefore it is considered by the Court that the Plaintiff recover against the Defendant and JAMES CRAIK, JUNR. his Security, one hundred pounds current money of Virginia, the Debt in the Declaration mentioned, together with their damages in form assessed and they costs by them about their suit in this behalf expended and the Defendant in mercy, &c.

Plaintiffs's costs   100 lbs tobacco @ 1 1/2   ]
                    70 lbs tobacco @ 1 1/4   ] p pound, & $10.77

Execution issued

    <u>Hodgson v Skinker</u>

    The Commonwealth of Virginia to the Sheriff of Prince William County, Greeting; We command you that you take WILLIAM SKINKER if he be found within your Bailiwick and him safely keep so that you have his body before the Judges of the District Court to be held at the Town of DUMFRIES at the next Court to answer WILLIAM HODGSON, Assignee of DAVID WILLSON SCOTT, who was Assignee of WILLIAM HEREFORD of a Plea of Debt for two hundred pounds, damage thirty pounds and have then there this Writ. Witness GEORGE BROOKE, Clerk of the Court at DUMFRIES the first day of September in the 15th year of the Commonwealth A. D. 1790

                G. BROOKE, C. D. D. C.

On a Bond for payment of money
Executed   JAMES TRIPLETT, D. Sh.
Prince William County, to wit
    WILLIAM HODGSON, Assignee of DAVID WILLSON SCOTT, who was
Assignee of WILLIAM HEREFORD complains of WILLIAM SKINKER in custody
and so forth of a Plea that he render to him the sum of two hundred pounds Virginia
currency which to him he owes and from him unjustly detains for this, to wit, that
whereas the Defendant on the second day of June in the year 1789

p.   Hodgson v Skinker
254   at the Parish of [blank] in the County aforesaid by his certain Writing Obliga-
        tory sealed with his seal and to the Court here now shewn the date whereof is
the same day and eyar aforesaid acknowledged himself to be held and firmly bound
unto WILLIAM HEREFORD in the sum of two hundred pounds Virginia currency to
be paid to him or his assigns; and whereas afterwards, to wit, on the 16th day of June
in the year 1789 at the Parish and County aforesaid assigned the Writing Obligatory
the same being then and there unpaid unto DAVID WILLSON SCOTT who on the
day and year last mentioned at the Parish and County assigned the Writing Obligatory the same being then and there unpaid unto the Plaintiff which Assignments are
severally written thereupon and of which the Defendant, viz. on the day and year last
mentioned at the Parish and County aforesaid had notice, by virtue of which premises
and the Act of Assembly in such case made, the Defendant became liable to pay to
the Plaintiff the sum of two hundred pounds Virginia currency; Nevertheless the Defendant though often required hat not paid to the Plaintiff the sum of money but hath
refused and still doth refuse to pay the same to him to his damage [blank] therefore
he sues, &c.
                                CHARLES LEE
        Pledges of prosecution John Doe & R. Roe
        November 1790   Bond & Declaration filed, Common Order against Defen-
                          dant and Sheriff
        December 1790   Common Order confirmed
        May 1791   Common Order set aside and payment
        Memorandum; that on the 14th day of May in the year of our Lord 1791 per-
sonally appeared before me, WILLOUGHBY TEBBS, a Justice of the Peace for
Prince William County, ALEXANDER BROWN and WILLIAM TYLER and undertook for WILLIAM SKINKER at the suit of [blank] HODGSON that if he should be
cast he should pay the costs and condemnation of the Court or render his body to
Prison in satisfaction for the same or that they, ALEXANDER BROWN and
WILLIAM TYLER, will do it for him; Given under my hand and seal the date above
                                WILLOUGHBY TEBBS

p.   Hodgson v Skinker
255   KNOW ALL MEN by these presents that I WILLIAM SKINKER of the
        County of Prince William and State of Virginia am held and firmly bound unto
WILLIAM HEREFORD of the Town of DUMFRIES and State aforesaid in the full
and just sum of two hundred pounds Virginia currency to be paid to WILLIAM
HEREFORD his heirs Executors Administrators or assigns, which payment well and

truly to be made and done I bind myself my heirs Executors Administrators and assigns firmly by these presents. dated the 2d of June 1789

THE CONDITION of the above obligation is such that if the above bound WILLIAM SKINKER his heirs Executors Administrators and assigns shall pay or cause to be paid on or before the tenth day of November next ensuing unto WILLIAM HEREFORD his heirs Executors Administrators or assigns the just sum of one hundred pounds secie in dollars at six shillings each or gold at five shillings and four pence the penny weight, then the above Obligation to be void or else to remain in full force and virtue, dated Prince William this 2d day of June 1789

Signed sealed and delivered in the presence of

WILLIAM DICKINSON   WM. SKINKER   [seal]

I do hereby assign the above bond to Mr. WILLIAM HODGSON or order for value received

DAVID WILLSON SCOTT

October 16, 1793

WILLIAM HODGSON, Assignee of DAVID WILLSON SCOTT   ]
who was Assignee of WILLIAM HEREFORD, Plaintiff   ]
          against   ]
WILLIAM SKINKER, Defendant   ]

This day came the parties by their Attornies and the Defendant relinquishing his former Plea acknowledged Plaintiff's action against him; therefore it is considered by the Court that the

p.   Hodgson v Skinker
256   Plaintiff recover against the Defendant two hundred pounds Virginia currency, the Debt in the Declaration mentioned and his costs by him about his suit in this behalf expended, and the Defendant in mercy, &c., But this Judgment may be discharged by payment of one hundred pounds specie in dollars at six shillings or gold at five shillings and four pence the penny weight with Interest thereon to be computed after the rate of five per centum per annum from the tenth day of November 1789 untill paid and the costs

Plaintiff's costs   100 lbs tobacco @ 1 1/2   ]
                       80 lbs tobacco @ 1 1/4   ] p pounds & $9.14.
Execution issued

Lewis & Bingham v Hough & Potts

The Commonwealth of Virginia to the Sheriff of LOUDOUN County Greeting; We command you as we have at another time commanded you that you take MAHLON HOUGH and JOHN POTTS if they be found in your Bailiwick and them safely keep so that you have them before the Judges of the District Court to be held at the Town of DUMFRIES at the next Court to answer MORDECAI LEWIS & WILLIAM BINGHAM, Assigness of WILLIAM HARTSHORNE, of a Plea of Debt for seven hundred seven pounds, eleven shillings and five pence half penny, damage ten pounds, and have then there this Writ. Witness GEORGE BROOKE, Clerk of the Court at DUMFRIES the 24th day of July in the 15th year of the Commonwealth A. D. 1790.

G. BROOKE, C. D. D. C.

For Debt due on Penal Bill, Bail is required
Executed on HOUGH and THOMAS HOUGH, Appearance Bail
POTTS not found   OSBORN KING, D. Sh.
LOUDOUN County, to wit
    MORDECAI LEWIS and WILLIAM BINGHAM Assignees of WILLIAM
HARTSHORNE, complain of MAHLON HOUGH and JOHN POTTS in custody, &c.
of a Plea that they render unto them the sum of seven hundred seven pounds, eleven
shillings and five pence two farthings current money of Virginia which to them they
owe and from them they unjustly detain for that whereas the Defendants on the
twenty sixth

p.   Lewis & Bingham v Hough & Potts
257   day of May in the year of our Lord one thousand seven hundred and eighty
        eight at the Parish and County aforesaid by their certain Writing Obligatory
sealed with their seals and to the Court here shewn the date whereof is on the same
day and year aforesaid did promise to pay to WILLIAM HARTSHORNE or order or
demand for value received the sum of three hundred fifty three pounds, fifteen
shillings and eight pence three farthings current money of Virginia to which payment
they bound themselves their heirs Executors and Administrators in the Penal sum of
seven hundred seven pounds, eleven shillings and five pence two farthings current
money and they, the Plaintiffs, in fact say the Defendants or either of them did not
pay to WILLIAM HARTSHORNE or order the sum of three hundred fifty three
pounds, fifteen shillings and five pence two farthings when they were thereunto afterwards required, to wit, the [blank] day of [blank] in the year 1783 which sum they
ought to have paid according to the form and effect of the Writing Obligatory whereby
an action accrued to WILLIAM HARTSHORNE to demand and have of the Defendants the sum of seven hundred seven pounds, eleven shilings and five pence two
farthings current money and whereas WILLIAM HARTSHORNE afterwards, to wit,
the fifth day of April in the year of our Lord one thousand seven hundred and eighty
eight at the Parish and County aforesaid the sum of seven hundred seven pounds,
eleven shillings and five pence two farthings current money being then and due and
unpaid assigned the Writing Obligatory to the Plaintiffs, MORDECAI LEWIS &
COMPANY which Company consists of MORDECAI LEWIS and WILLIAM BING-
HAM, for value received by his certain writing indorsed on the back of the Writing
Obligatory signed by WILLIAM HARTSHORNE of which Assignment the Defendants the day year and place last mentioned had notice by virtue whereof and by
force of the Act of Assembly in such cases made and provided, an action accrued to
the Plaintiffs to demand and have of the Defendants the last mentioned sum of
money, yet the Defendants altho often required the sum

p.   Lewis & Bingham v Hough & Potts
258   of money or any penny thereof have not paid to the Plaintiffs but the same to
        them to pay hath altogether refused and still doth refuse to the damage of the
Plaintiffs ten pounds, and therefore they bring suit &c.
                                SIMMS for Plaintiffs

    Pledges &c. J. Doe & R. Roe
    June 1790   Alias capias

November 1790   Common Order against HOUGH and plurias capias
                                    against POTTS
December 1790   Common Order continued against HOUGH
May 1791   Common Order set aside and Payment for Security
October 1793   Judgment confirmed by HOUGH

    KNOW ALL MEN by these presents that we MAHLON HOUGH and THO-
MAS HOUGH of LOUDOUN County are held and firmly bound unto JAMES COLE-
MAN, Gentleman, Sheriff of the County, in the full and just sum of one thousand four
hundred fifteen pounds, two shillings and five pence half penny, to which payment well
and truly to be made and done we bind ourselves and each of our Executors Adminis-
trators jointly and severally firmly by these presents, Sealed with our seals and dated
the 2d day of September 1790
    THE CONDITION of the above Obligation is such that if the above bound MAH-
LON HOUGH shall an do make his personal appearance before the Judges of the
District Court to be held at the Town of DUMFRIES at the next Court to answer
MORDECAI LEWIS and WILLIAM BINGHAM, Assignees of WILLIAM HARTS-
HORNE & COMPANY, of a Plea of Debt for seven hundred seven pounds, eleven
shillings and five pence half penny, damage ten pounds, that then the above Obligation to be void or else to remain in full force and virtue
Sealed and delivered in the presence of
    OSBORN KING   MAHLON HOUGH   [seal]
                                      THOMAS HOUGH   [seal]
    We promise to pay to WILLIAM HARTSHORNE or order on demand the sum
of three hundred fifty three pounds, fifteen shillings and eight pence three farthings in
silver dollars at six shillings each or other silver or gold of equal value for value received, to which payment we bind ourselves our heirs Executors and Administrators
in the penal sum of

p.   Lewis & Bingham v Hough & Potts
259   seven hundred seven pounds, eleven shillings and 5 1/2 like money as above;
    Witness our hands and seals this twenty sixth day of May in the year one thou-
sand seven hundred and eighty eight.
Sealed and delivered in presence of
    JNO: BEALLE   HOUGH & POTTS   [seal]
    I assign the within Note to MORDECAI LEWIS & CO. for value received
April 5th 1790

                       WILLIAM HARTSHORNE
October 16th 1793
    MORDECAI LEWIS & WILLIAM BINGHAM, Assignees]
    of WILLIAM HARTSHORNE, Plaintiffs   ]
          against   ] In Debt
    MAHLON HOUGH & JOHN POTTS, Defendants   ]
    This day came as well the Plaintiffs by heir Attorney as the Defendant MAHLON
HOUGH by his Attorney and the Defendant relinquishing his former Plea acknowledged the Plaintiffs's action against him; therefore it is considered by the Court that
the Plaintiffs recover against the Defendant and THOMAS HOUGH, his Security,

seven hundred seven pounds, eleven shillings and five pence half penny in silver dollars at six shillings each or other silver or gold of equal value, the Debt in the Declaration mentioned, and their costs by them about their suit in this behalf expended, and the Defendant in mercy, &c., But this Judgment may be discharged by the payment of three hundred fifty three pounds, fifteen shillings and eight pence three farthings like money with Interest thereon to be computed after the rate of five per centum per annum from the 26th day of May 1788 untill paid and the costs. The Defendant is to have Credit for all discounts which shall be made appear to JOHN FITZGERALD on or before the first day of January next

Plaintiffs's costst   185 lbs tobacco @ 1 1/2   ]
                          200 lbs tobacco @ 1 1/4   ] p pound & $8.56

Execution issued

p.   **Murray & Co. v Love**
260   The Commonwealth of Virginia to the Sheriff of Prince William County, Greeting. We command you that you take JOHN LOVE if he be found within your Bailiwick and him safely keeep so that you have him before the Judges of the District Court to be held at the Town of DUMFRIES at the next Court to answer JOHN MURRAY & COMPANY of a Plea of Debt for six thousand seven hundred and ninety five pounds of crop tobacco, damage twenty pounds, and have then there this Writ. Witness GEORGE BROOKE, Clerk of the Court at DUMFRIES the 28th day of July in the 15th year of the Commonwealth A.D. 1790
.G. BROOKE C.D.C.
For tobacco due on Promissory Note, Bail is required
Executed   GEO. G. TYLER, D Sh.
FAUQUIER County to wit;
JOHN MURRAY & COMPANY complain of JOHN LOVE in custody, &c. of a Plea that he render unto them the quantity of six thousand seven hundred ninety five pounds of crop tobacco with Interest thereon which to them he owes and from them unjustly detains for that whereas the Defendant on the 27th day of December in the year 1788 at the Town of ALEXANDRIA in the Parish of [blank] and County aforesaid by his certain writing with his proper hand and name thereto subscribed commonly called a Promissory Note for value received did promise to pay to the Plaintiffs or their order the quantity of six thousand seven hundred ninety five pounds crop tobacco of the present Inspection at DUMFRIES in six weeks from the date thereof with Interest after that time till paid and the Plaintiffs in fact say that the Defendant did not pay to them or to either of them or to their order the quantity of crop tobacco at DUMFRIES within six weeks from the date of the writing which he ought to have paid to the Plaintiffs within the time according to the form and effect of the writing, whereby an action accrued to the Plaintiffs to demand and have of the Defendant the quantity of crop tobacco with Interest thereon as aforesaid, yet the Defendant altho often

p.   **Murray & Co. v Love**
261   required, the quantity of tobacco with Interest thereon to the Plaintiffs or either of them hath paid but the same to them to pay hath altogether refused and still doth refuse to the damage of the Plaintiffs [blank] pounds, therefore they bring suit, &c.   SIMMS for the Plaintiffs

Pledges for prosecution J. Doe & R. Roe
November 1790   Bail filed, Common Order
December 1790   Declaration filed, Common Order confirmed
May 1791   Common Order set aside and payment
    Memorandum; that on the 18th day of May in the year one thousand seven
hundred and ninety one personally appeared before me, JESSE EWELL , a Justice of
the Peace for the County of Prince William, WILLIAM TYLER of the County afore-
said and undertook for JOHN LOVE at the suit of JOHN MURRAY & COMPANY,
Merchants in ALEXANDRIA, in an action of Debt depending in the District Court at
DUMFRIES that in case JOHN LOVE should be cast in this suit he, JOHN LOVE,
will pay and satisfy the condemnation of the Court or render his body to Prison in
Execution for the same or that he, WILLIAM TYLER, will do it for him; Given under
my hand and seal the day and year above written
                                    JESSE EWELL
    For value received, I promise to pay to JOHN MURRAY & CO. or their order
six thousand seven hundred ninety five pounds of crop tobacco of the present Inspection at DUMFRIES in six months from this date with Interest after that time till paid
Witness my hand in ALEXANDRIA December 27th 1788
    6795 pounds Crop tobacco   JNO: LOVE
October 16th 1793
    JOHN MURRAY & COMPANY, Plaintiffs   ]
              against   ] In Debt
    JOHN LOVE, Defendant   ]
    This day came the parties by their Attornies and the Defendant relinquishing his
former Plea acknowledged the Plaintiffs action

p.   Murray & Co. v Love
262   against him; therefore it is considered by the Court that the Plaintiffs recover
          against the Defendant six thousand seven hundred ninety five pounds of crop
tobacco of the present Inspection at DUMFRIES with Interest thereon to be computed after the rate of five per centum per annum from the twenty seventh day of
December 1788 untill paid, the Debt in the Declaration mentioned, and their costs by
them about their suit in this behalf expended and the Defendant in mercy, &c
    Plaintiffs's costs   85 lbs tobacco @ 1 1/2   ]
                         40 lbs tobacco @ 1 1/4   ] p pound & $7.58.

        Stuart & Love v Lowe
    The Commonwealth of Virginia to the Sheriff of LOUDOUN County, Greeting.
We command you that you take HENRY LOWE if he be found within your Bailiwick
and him safely keep so that you have him before the Judges of the District Court to
be held at the Town of DUMFRIES at the next Court to answer HUGH STUART and
SAMUEL LOVE of a Plea of Debt for forty pounds, damage five pounds, and to have
then and there this Writ. Witness GEORGE BROOKE, Clerk of the Court at DUM-
FRIES the 21st day of September in the 15th year of the Commonwealth A. D. 1790
                                    G. BROOKE, C. D. C.

On a Penal Bill, Bail is required
Executed and JOSEPH EVERETT Appearance Bail
F. ADAMS, D. S. L. C.

LOUDOUN County, to wit

HUGH STUART and SAMUEL LOVE complain of [blank] LOWE in custody
&c. of a Plea &c. that he render unto them the sum of forty pounds which to them he
owes and from them unjustly detains for that whereas the Defendant upon the seventeenth day of May in the year of our Lord one thousand seven hundred and ninety at
the Parish and County aforesaid by his certain Penal Bill in writing with his own hand
sealed with his seal and here into Court produced bearing date the same day and year
aforesaid bound himself to pay to the Plaintiffs the sum of nineteen pounds, four shillings and one penny to be paid to the Plaintiffs on demand and for the same payment
well and truly to be made he, the Defendant, by the Bill firmly bound himself his heirs
Executors and Administrators in the aforesaid penal

p.   Stuart & Love v Lowe
263   sum of forty pounds and the Plaintiffs in fact do aver that the Defendant the
        nineteen pounds, four shillings and four pence aforesaid unto them unto them
the Plaintiffs on demand did not pay which he ought to have paid to them according to
the tenor and effect of the Bill whereby an action accrued to the Plaintiffs to have and
demand of the Defendant the sum of forty pounds, yet the Defendant altho thereunto
often required hath not yet paid the forty pounds to the Plaintiffs but the same to pay
hitherto hath refused and doth refuse to the damage of the Plaintiffs five pounds and
therefore they bring suit, &c.
                                    M. HARRISON for Plaintiffs

For the Plaintiffs   [J. Doe
Pledges &c   ] R. Roe
November 1790   Common Order against Defendant & Security
December 1790   Bail filed, Common Order set aside & oyer
January 1791   Rule to plead
February 1791   Continued for Plea
March 1791   ditto
April 1791   Judgment by default
May 1791   Judgment set aside and payment

KNOW ALL MEN by these presents that we HENRY LOWE and JOSEPH
EVERETT of the County of LOUDOUN are held and firmly bound unto JAMES
COLEMAN, Gent., Sheriff for the County, in the full and just sum of eighty pounds to
which payment well and truly to be made and done we bind ourselves our and each of
our heirs Executors and Administrators jointly and severally firmly by these presents
Sealed with our seals and dated the 30th of September 1790
THE CONDITION of the above Obligation is such that if the above bound
HENRY LOWE shall and so make his personal appearance before the Judges of the
District Court to be held in DUMFRIES the first day of next Court to answer HUGH
STUART and SAMUEL LOVE of a Plea of Debt for forty pounds, damage five
pounds, that then the above Obligation to be void or else to remain in full force and

virtue &c.
Sealed and deliverd in presence of
  F. ADAMS, D. S.   HENRY LOWE [seal]
            JOSEPH EVERETT [seal]

p. Stuart & Love v Lowe
264 Memorandum; That upon the 1st day of October 1790 personally appeared
before me, PATRICK CAVAN, Gentleman, a Justice of the Peace for the
County of LOUDOUN, JOHN GEST of the County aforesaid and undertook for
HENRY LOWE at the suit of SAMUEL LOVE in an action of Debt now depending in
the District Court of DUMFRIES, that in case HENRY LOWE shall be cast in this
suit he, HENRY LOWE, will pay and satisfy the condemnation of the Court or render
his body to Prison in Execution for the same or that he, JOHN GEST, will do it for
him;

         PATK. CAVAN
  I HENRY LOWE of the County of LOUDON do oblige myself my heirs Executors and Administrators to pay or cause to be paid on demand unto HUGH STUART
and SAMUEL LOVE, both of the County aforesaid, the just sum of nineteen pounds,
four shillings and one penny to be paid in English French of Spanish gold at five shillngs and four pence the penny weight or in silver dollars at six shillings each with legal
Interest thereon till paid it being for value received, to the which payment well and
truly to be made I bind myself my heirs Executors and Administrators jointly and
severally by these presents in the penal sum of forty pounds like money. In Witness
whereof I have hereunto set my hand and seal this 7th day of May 1790
Signed sealed and delivered in the presence of
ALEXANDER GALLOWAY   HENRY LOWE [seal]

October 16th 1793
  HUGH STUART & SAMUEL LOVE, Plaintiffs   ]
     against   ] In Debt
  HENRY LOWE, Defendant   ]
  This day came the parties by their Attornies and the Defendant relinquishing his
former Plea acknowledged the Plaintiffs's action against him; therefore it is considered that the Plaintiffs recover against the Defendant forty pounds in English
French or Spanish gold at five shillings and four pence the penny weight or in silver
dollars at six shillings each, the Debt in the Declaration mentioned, and their costs by
them about their suit in this behalf expended, and the Defendant in mercy, &c., But
this Judgment may be discharged by the payment of nineteen pounds, four shillings
and one penny like money with Interest thereon to be computed after the rate of five
per centum per annum from the 17th day of May 1790 untill paid and the costs
  Plaintiffs's costs 9/ 55 lbs tobacco @ 1 1/2]
        70 lbs tobacco @ 1 1/4] p pound & $4.44.
  Execution issued

p.   Scott & Co. v Tackett
265   The Commonwealth of Virginia to the Sheriff of Prince William County,
        Greeting. We command you as we have at another time commanded you to
take WILLIAM TACKETT if he be found within your Bailiwick and him safely keep
so that you have his body before the Judges of the District Court to be held at the
Town of DUMFRIES at the next Court to answer DAVID WILLSON SCOTT & CO.
of a Plea of Debt for fifty pounds gold or silver, damage five pounds, and have then and
there this Writ. Witness GEORGE BROOKE, Clerk of the Court at DUMFRIES the
31st day of July in the 15th year of the Commonwealth, A. D. 1790.
                                        G. BROOKE, C. D. C.
        For Debt due by Bond, Bail is required
        Executed   JAMES TRIPLETT, D. S.
Prince William County, to wit
        DAVID WILLSON SCOTT & COMPANY complain of WILLIAM TACKETT in
custody &c., of a Plea &c., that he render unto them the sum of fifty pounds gold or
silver which to them he owes and from them unjustly detains for that whereas
WILLIAM TACKETT on the 29th day of October in the year of our Lord one thousand seven hundred and eighty seven at the Parish of Dettingen in the County aforesaid by his certain Writing Obligatory sealed with his seal and now produced in Court
the date whereof is the day and year aforesaid, acknowledged himself to be bound to
DAVID WILLSON SCOTT & CO. in the sum of fifty pounds gold or silver to be paid
to DAVID WILLSON SCOTT & CO. when he, WILLIAM, should thereunto afterwards be required, Nevertheless WILLIAM tho often required hath not paid the fifty
pounds gold or silver to the Plaintiff but the same to pay hath refused and still doth
refuse to the damage of the Plaintiff five pounds, and therefore they bring suit, &c.
                                        DADE p Plaintiffs
        Pledges J. Doe & R. Roe
        November 1790   Common Order against Defendant & Sheriff
        December 1790   Common Order confirmed
        May 1791   Common Order set aside and payment for Sheriff
Prince William County, Sct.
        Memorandum: That on the fourteenth day of October 1791, personally
appeared before me, JESSE EWELL, one of the

p.   Scott & Co. v Tackett
266   Justices of Prince William County, GEORGE PURCELL and undertook to
        become Special Bail for WILLIAM TACKETT at the suit of DAVID WILLSON
SCOTT & CO., in the District Court that if WILLIAM TACKETT should be cast in
this suit he should pay the condemnation of the Court or render his body to Prison or
that he, GEORGE PURCELL, should do it for him; Acknowledged before me the date
above written
                                        JESSE EWELL
        KNOW ALL MEN by these presents that I WILLIAM TACKETT of Prince
William County and State of Virginia am held and firmly bound unto WILLIAM
SCOTT & CO. of the County and Town of DUMFRIES in the just and full sum of fifty
pounds gold or silver for value received to be paid to DAVID WILLSON SCOTT & CO.
and their certain Attorney their heirs Executors Administrators or assigns on or

before the first day of January next as witness my hand and seal this 29th dy of October 1787

THE CONDITION of the above Obligation is such that if the above bound WILLIAM TACKETT shall well and truly pay or cause to be paid unto DAVID WILLSON SCOTT & CO. their certain Attorney their heirs Executors Administrators or assigns the just and full sum of twenty five pounss in gold or silver on or before the first day of January next ensuing the date hereof then the above Obligation to be void or else to remain in full force and virtue in Law

Test THOMAS MARSHALL,   WILLIAM TACKETT [seal]
        JAMES his mark _/_ WILLIAMS
October 16th 1793
            DAVID WILLSON SCOTT & CO., Plaintiffs   ]
                    against   ] In Debt
            WILLIAM TACKETT, Defendant   ]

This day came the parties by their Attornies and the Defendant relinquishing his former Plea acknowledged the Plaintiffs's action against him; therefore it is considered by the Court that the Plaintiffs recover against the Defendant and JAMES TRIPLETT, Deputy Sheriff of Prince William County, fifty pounds gold or silver, the Debt in the Declaration mentioned, and their costs by them about their suit in this behalf expended, and the Defendant in mercy, &c. But this Judgment may be

p.   Scott & Co. v Tackett
267   discharged by the payment of twenty five pounds in gold or silver with Interest thereon to be computed after the rate of five percentum per annum from the first day of January 1788 untill paid and the costs. The Defendant is to have Credit for four shillings and eleven pence half penny

            Plaintiffs's costs   125 lbs tobacco @ 1 1/2   ]
                                  70 lbs tobacco @ 1 1/4   ] p pound & $7.17

            Execution issued

            Lee v Love
    The Commonwealth of Virginia to the Sheriff of Prince William County Greeting. We command you that you take JOHN LOVE if he be found within your Bailiwick and him safely keep so that you have his body before the Judges of the District Court to be held at the Town of DUMFRIES at the next Court to answer HENRY LEE, Esquire, of a Plea of Debt for one thousand pounds, damage ten pounds and have then there this Writ. Witness GEORGE BROOKE, Clerk of the Court at DUMFRIES the 23d day of April in the 14th year of the Commonwealth A.D. 1790
                            G. BROOKE, C. D. D. C.
            Executed GEORGE G. TAYLOR, D, Sh.
Prince William County, to wit;
    HENRY LEE complains of JOHN LOVE in custody and so forth of a Plea that he render to him the sum of one thousand pounds lawful money of Virginia which to him he owes and from him unjustly detains for this to wit tht whereas the Defendant on the fifteenth day of December in the year 1788 at the Parish of [blank] in the Coun-

ty aforesaid by his certain Writing Obligatory sealed with his seal and to the Court now here shewn the date whereof is on the same day and year acknowledged himself to be held and firmly bound unto the Plaintiff in the sum of one thousand pounds lawful money of Virginia to be paid to the Plaintiff when reqired; Nevertheless the Defendant tho often afterwards required hath not paid to the Plaintiff the one thousand pounds lawful money but hath refused and still doth refuse to pay the same to him to his damage ten pounds and therefore he brings this suit, &c.

CHARLES LEE for Plaintiff

Pledges of Prosecution, J. Doe & R. Roe

p.   Lee v Love
268   June 1790   Common Order against Defendant and Sheriff
            July 1790   Common Order confirmed
            October 1790   Common Order set aside and payment

Memorandum; that on the 23d day of September in the year of our Lord one thousand seven hundred and ninety SAMUEL LOVE of the County of Prince William personally appeared before me, FRANCIS TRIPLETT, Gent., a Justice of the Peace for FAUQUIER County and undertook for JOHN LOVE at the suit of HENRY LEE in an action of Debt now depending in the District Court at the Town of DUMFRIES, that in case JOHN LOVE shall be cast in the suit he, JOHN LOVE, will pay and satisfy the condemnation of the Court or render his body to Prison in Execution for the same or that he, SAMUEL LOVE, will do it for him; Given under my hand and seal the day and year aforesaid

FRANCIS TRIPLETT   [seal]

KNOW ALL MEN by these presents that I JOHN LOVE of the County of Prince William and State of Virginia am held and firmly bound to HENRY LEE of the County of WESTMORELAND and State of Virginia in the just and full sum of one thousand pounds lawful money of Virginia to be paid to HENRY LEE his heirs Executors Administrators or assigns for the which payment well and truly to be made I bind myself my heirs Executors and Administrators firmly by these presents; Sealed with my seal and dated the 15th day of December 1788

THE CONDITION of the above Obligation is such that if the above bound JOHN LOVE shall and do well and truly pay or cause to be paid unto HENRY LEE the just and full sum of five hundred pounds like money on demand with Interest then this Obligation to be void or else to remain in full force and virtue in the Law Signed sealed and delivered in presence of

RICHARD M. SCOTT   JOHN LOVE   [seal]
October 16th 1793

HENRY LEE, Esqr. Plaintiff   ]
          against   ] In Debt
JOHN LOVE, Defendant   ]

This day came the parties by their Attornies and the Defendant relinquishing his former Plea ackowledged the Plaintiff's action against him; therefore it is

p.   Lee v Love
269   considered by the Court that the Plaintiff recover against the Defendant one thousand pounds lawfull money, the Debt in the Declaration mentioned, and

his costs by him about his suit in this behalf expended and the Defendant in mercy, &c., But this Judgment may be discharged by payment of five hundred pounds like money with Interest thereon to be computed after the rate of five per centum per annum from the fifteenth day of December 1788 untill paid and the costs

Plaintiff's costs   125 lbs tobacco @ 1 1/2   ]
60 lbs tobacco @ 1 1/4   ] p pound & $7.58

October 21st 1793

The Plaintiff by his Attorney acknowledged the Receipt of the three hundred and nine pounds in part of a Judgment obtained against the Defendant this term and agrees to stay Execution for the balance twelve months

Wattson & Co. v Greenway & Hunter

The Commonwealth of Virginia to the Sheriff of FAIRFAX County, Greeting We command you that you take JOSEPH GREENWAY and WILLIAM HUNTER. SENR. if they be found within your Bailiwich and them safely keep so that you have their bodies before the Judges of the District Court to be held at the Town of DUM-FRIES at the next Court to answer JOSIAH WATTSON & COMPANY, Assignees of JONATHAN SWIFT of a Plea of Debt for two hundred pounds, damage two pounds, and have then there this Writ. Witness GEORGE BROOKE, Clerk of the Court at DUMFRIES the 15th day of May in the 14th year of the Commonwealth A. D. 1790

G. BROOKE, C. D. C.

For Debt due by Bond, Bail is required

Executed, Capt. JOHN HARPER, DENNIS RAMSAY and LEWIS WESTON Appearance Bail

CHARLES TURNER, D Sh.

FAIRFAX, to wit

JOSIAH WATTSON & COMPANY, Assignees of JONATHAN SWIFT, com-plain of JOSEPH GREENWAY and WILLIAM HUNTER, SENR. of a Plea that they render unto them the sum of two hundred pounds Virginia currency which to them they owe and from them unjustly detain &c. for this to wit

p.   ### Wattson & Co. v Greenway & Hunter
270   that the Defendants on the seventeenth day of July in the year of our Lord one thousand seven hundred and eighty seven at the Parish of Fairfax in the County aforesaid by their certain Writing Obligatory sealed with the seal of the De-fendants and to the Court here now shewn, the date whereof is on the day and year aforesaid, did acknowledge themselves to be hald and firmly bound unto JONATHAN SWIFT in the sum of two hundred pounds Virginia currency to which payment well and truly to be made unto JONATHAN SWIFT or to his Attorney, Executors Ad-ministrators or assigns they bound themselves their heirs Executors and Administra-tors by the Writing Obligatory and JONATHAN SWIFT, to wit on the [blank] day of [blank] in the year of our Lord 1788 at the Parish aforesaid in the County aforesaid the sum of money then being due and unpaid by his certain writing endorsed on the back of the Writing Obligatory and signed subscribed with the proper hand and anme of JONATHAN SWIFT assigned the Writing Obligatory to the Plaintiffs for value re-

ceived of which Assignment the Defendants afterwards, to wit, on the day and year last mentioned, at the Parish and County aforesaid, had notice by virtue of which Assignment and by force of the Act of Assembly in such cases made and provided action accrued to the Plaintiffs to demand and have of the Defendants the sum of money; Nevertheless the Defendants altho often required the sum of money to the Plaintiffs have not paid but the same to them to pay hitherto have refused and still do refuse to the damage of the Plaintiffs [blank] pounds, and thereupon they bring suit,&c.

SIMMS for the Plaintiffs

Pledges &c. J. Doe & R. Roe

November 1790	Common Order against Defendant and Security
December 1790	Declaration filed and Common Order confirmed
May 1791	Common Order set aside and payment for Security
October 1793	Judgment

p. 271   Wattson & Co. v Greenway & Hunter

KNOW ALL MEN by these presents that we JOSEPH GREENWAY and WILLIAM HUNTER, SENR. JOHN HARPER, DENNIS RAMSAY and LEWIS WESTON of FAIRFAX County and State of Virginia are held and firmly bound unto ROBERT TOWNSHEND HOOE, Sheriff of the County, in the just and full sum of four hundred four pounds current money of Virginia to which payment well and truly to be made we bind ourselves and each of us our and each of our heirs Executors and Administrators jointly and severally firmly by these presents; Sealed with our seals and dated this 16th day of May 1790

Whereas JOSIAH WATTSON & COMPANY, Assignees of JONATHAN SWIFT, hath sued forth against JOSEPH GREENWAY and WILLIAM HUNTER, SENR. out of the District Court held at DUMFRIES a Writ of capias ad respondendum in a Plea of Debt for two hundred pounds, damage two pounds, directed to the Sheriff of the County of FAIRFAX which hath been executed upon JOSEPH GREENWAY and WILLIAM HUNTER, SENR.

Now the Condition of the above Obligation is such that if the above bound JOSEPH GREENWAY and WILLIAM HUNTER, SENR. do make their personal appearance at the next Court to be held for the District at the Courthouse in DUMFRIES on the [blank] day of May Term and do then and there abide by fulfill and perform such Orders as by the Court shall be made in the action and do not depart from the Court till the same shall be performed, then the above Obligation to be void or else to remain in full force and virtue in Law

Signed and delivered in presence of

CHARLES TURNER

JOSEPH GREENWAY [seal]
WILLIAM HUNTER [seal]
JOHN HARPER [seal]
DENNIS RAMSAY [seal]
LEWIS WESTON [seal]

Memorandum; That upon the twelfth day of october in the year of our Lord one thousand seven hundred and ninety JOHN HARPER and DENNIS RAMSAY of the County of FAIRFAX personally appeared before me, JOHN FITZGERALD, Gentleman, one of the Justices of the Peace for the County and authorized for taking

Special Bail within the County of FAIRFAX and undertook for

p.   Wattson & Co. v Greenway & Hunter
272   JOSEPH GREENWAY at the suit of JOSIAH WATTSON in [blank] now
        depending in the Honourable District Court at DUMFRIES that in case
JOSEPH GREENWAY shall be cast in the suit he, JOSEPH GREENWAY, will pay
and satisfy the condemnatiion of the Court or render his body to Prison in Execution
for the same or that they, JOHN HARPER and DENNIS RAMSAY will do it for him,
Acknowledged before

                              JOHN FITZGERALD
        KNOW ALL MEN by these presents that we JOSEPH GREENWAY and
WILLIAM HUNTER, SENR. of the Town of ALEXANDRIA, State of Virginia, Merchants, are held and firmly bound unto JONATHAN SWIFT & COMPANY of the
Town and State aforesaid in the full and just sum of two hundred pounds Virginia
currency to be paid to JONATHAN SWIFT or to his certain Attorney Executors,
Administrators or assigns to the which payment well and truly to be made we bind
ourselves heirs Executors Administrators and each of them firmly by these presents,
Sealed with our seals and dated the 17th day of July in the year of our Lord one thousand seven hundred and eighty seven
        THE CONDITION of the above Obligation is such that if the above bound
JOSPEH GREENWAY and WILLIAM HUNTER, SENR. do and shall well and truly
pay or cause to be paid unto JONATHAN SWIFT or to his certain Attorney Executors Administrators or assigns the full and just sum of one hundred pounds in gold or
silver at or upon the seventeenth day of January 1789 with lawful Interest for the
same then the above Obigation to be void or else to remain in full force and virtue in
Law
Sealed and delivered in presence of
        JOHN DUNLAP   JOS: GREENWAY   [seal]
        LEVIN C. WAILES   WM. HUNTER   [seal]

        Debt   L.   100.....0.....0
        Interest to 28 Decembe5 1789   12....5....0
                                       L   112.....5.....0
        Received at different times as pr Receipts   L   42....6....0
        Pounds 70 due 28th December 1789

p.   Wattson & Co. v Greenway & Hunter
273   Pay the above to Messrs. JOSIAH WATTSON & CO. or order to whom I
        assign all my right and title to the within for value received
                              JONATHAN SWIFT
Octobe 17th 1793
        JOSIAH WATTSON & COMPANY, Assignees of   ]
        JONATHAN SWIFT, Plaintiffs   ]
                against   ]   In Debt
        JOSEPH GREENWAY & WILLIAM HUNTER, Defendants   ]
     This day came the parties by their Attornies and this suit abates as to the De-
fendant WILLIAM HUNTER, SENR. by his death and the surviving Defendant

relinquishing his former Plea acknowledged the Plaintiffs's action against him; therefore it is considered by the Court that the Plaintiffs recover against the Defendant two hundred pounds Virginia currency, the Debt in the Declaration mentioned, and their costs by them about their suit in this behalf expended and the Defendant in mercy &c., But this Judgment may be discharged by the payment of one hundred pounds in gold or silver with Interest thereon to be computed after the rate of five per centum per annum from the seventeenth day of July 1787 untill paid and the costs

Plaintiffs's costs   130 lbs tobacco @ 1 1/2   ]
                         75 lbs tobacco @ 1 1/4   ] p pound & $7.98.
                                                     Execution   .40 $8.38

Wattson & Co. v Greenway & Hunter

The Commonwealth of Virginia to the Sheriff of FAIRFAX County, Greeting. We command you that you take JOSEPH GREENWAY & WILLIAM HUNTER, SENR. if they be found within your Bailiwick and them safely keep so that you have them before the Judges of the District Court to be held at the Town of DUMFRIES at the next Court to answer JOSIAH WATTSON & COMPANY, Assignees of JONATHAN SWIFT, of a Plea of Debt for two hundred pounds, damage two pounds, and hve then there this Writ. Witness GEORGE BROOKE, Clerk of the Court at DUMFRIES the 15th day of May in the 14th year of the Commonwealth A.D. 1790

                                        G. BROOKE, C. D. C.

For Debt due by bond. Bail is required

Executed Capt. JOHN HARPER, DENNIS RAMSAY and LEWIS WESTON Appearance Bail

                          CHARLES TURNER, D. S.

p.   ### Wattson & Co. v Greenway and Hunter
274   FAIRFAX to wit.   JOSIAH WATTSON & COMPANY, Assignees of JONATHAN SWIFT, complain of JOSEPH GREENWAY and WILLIAM HUNTER, SENR. of a Plea that they render unto them the sum of two hundred pounds Virginia currency which to them they owe and from them unjustly detain and so forth for this to wit that the Defendants on the seventeenth day of July in the year of our Lord one thousand seven hundred and eighty seven at the Parish of Fairfax in the County aforesaid by their certain Writing Obligatory sealed with the seals of the Defendants and to the Court now here shewn, the date whereof is the same day and year aforesaid, did acknowledge themselves to be held and firmly bound unto JONATHAN SWIFT in the sum of two hundred pounds Virginia currency to which payment well and truly to be made unto JONATHAN SWIFT or to his certain Attorney, Executors Adminsitrators of assigns to which payment well and truly to be made they bound themselves their heirs Executors and Administrators firmly by the Writing Obligatory and JONATHAN SWIFT afterwards on the [blank] day of [blank] in the year of our Lord one thousand seven hundred and eighty eight at the Parish and County aforesaid the sum of money being wholly due and unpaid for value received by his certain writing endoresed on the Writing Obligatory signed and subscribed with the proper hand and name of JONATHAN SWIFT assigned the Writing Obligatory unto

the Plaintiffs of which Assignment the Defendants afterwards, to wit, on the day and year last mentiioned at the Parish and County aforesaid has notice by virtue of which Assignment and force of the Act of Assembly in such cases made and provided, action accrued to the Plaintiff to demand and have of the Defendants the sum of two hundred pounds Virginia currency, Nevertheless the Defendants altho often required the sum of two hundred pounds to the Plaintiffs have not apid but the same to pay hitherto have refused and still do refuse to the damage of the Plaintiffs [blank] pounds, and thereupon they bring suit &c.

SIMMS for the Plaintiffs

Pledges &c. J. Doe & R. Roe.
November 1790   Common Order against Defendants and Security
December 1790   Declaration filed, Common Order confirmed
May 1791   Common Order set aside and payment

p. 275   Wattson & Co. v Greenway & Hunter

KNOW ALL MEN by these presents tht we JOSEPH GREENWAY and WILLIAM HUNTER, SENR. JOHN HARPER, DENNIS RAMSAY and LEWIS WESTON of FAIRFAX County and State of Virginia are held and firmly bound unto ROBERT TOWNSHEND HOOE, Gent., Sheriff of FAIRFAX County, in the just and full sum of four hundred and four pounds current money of Virginia to be aid unto ROBERT T. HOOE his Executors, Administrators or assigns, to which payment well and truly to be made we bind ourselves and each of us our and each of our heirs Executors and Administrators jointly and severally firmly by these presents; Sealed with our seals and dated the 16th day of May 1790

Whereas JOSIAH WATTSON & COMPANY, Assignees of JONATHAN SWIFT, hath sued forth against JOSEPH GREENWAY and WILLIAM HUNTER, SENR. out of the District Court held at DUMFRIES a Writ of capias ad respondendum in a Plea of Debt for two hundred pounds, damage two pounds, directed unto the Sheriff of the County of FAIRFAX which hath been executed upon JOSEPH GREENWAY and WILLIAM HUNTER, SENR.

Now the Condition of the above Obligation is such that if the above bound JOSEPH GREENWAY and WILLIAM HUNTER, SENR. do make their personal appearance at the next District Court to be held at the Courthouse in DUMFRIES the [blank] day of May Term and do then and there abide by fulfill and perform such Orders as by the Court shall be made in the action and do not depart from the Court till the same is performed then the above Obligation to be void or else to remain in full force and virtue in the Law
Signed and delivered in presence of
CHARLES TURNER

JOSEPH GREENWAY [seal]
WM. HUNTER [seal]
JOHN HARPER [seal]
DENNIS RAMSAY [seal]
LEWIS WESTON [seal]

KNOW ALL MEN by these presents that we JOSEPH GREENWAY and WILLIAM HUNTER, SENR. of the Town of ALEXANDRIA, State of Virginia, Merchants, are held and firmly bound unto JONATHAN SWIFT of the Town and State aforesaid in the full and just sum of two hundred pounds Virginia currency to be paid unto JONATHAN SWIFT or to his certain Attorney Executors Administrators

p.   Wattson & Co. v Greenway & Hunter
276   or assigns to the which payment well and truly to be made and done we bind
        ourselves heirs Executors and Administrators and each of them firmly by
these presents; sealed with our seals and dated this 17th day of July in the year of our
Lord one thousand seven hundred and eighty seven
    THE CONDITION of the above Obligation is such that if the above bound
JOSEPH GREENWAY & WILLIAM HUNTER, SENR. do and shall well and truly
pay or cause to be paid unto JONATHAN SWIFT or to his certain Attorney Executors Administrators or assigns the full and just sum of one hundred pounds in gold or
silver at or upon the seventeenth day of January 1790 with lawful Interest for the
same then the above Obligation to be void else to remain in full force and virtue in
Law
Sealed and delivered in presence of
    JOHN DUNLAP   JOS: GREENWAY   [seal]
    LEVIN C. WAILES   WM. HUNTER   [seal]

    Debt   L.   100.....0.....0
    Interest to 28th December 1789   L   12.....5.....0
                                     L   112.....5.....0
    Pay the above to J. WATTSON & CO. or Order to whom I assign all my right
and title to the within, value received
                                JONATHAN SWIFT
October 17th 1793
    JOSIAH WATTSON & CO. Assignees of   ]
    JONATHAN SWIFT, Plaintiffs   ]
            against   ] In Debt
    JOSEPH GREENWAY & WILLIAM HUNTER, Defendants   ]
    This day came the parties by their Attornies and this suit abates as to the De-
fendant, WILLIAM HUNTER, SENR. by his death and the surviving Defendant relinquishing his former Plea acknowledged the Plaintiffs's action against him; therefore
it is considered by the Court that the Plaintiffs recover against the Defendant two
hundred pounds Virginia currency, the Debt in the Declaration mentioned, and their
costs by them about their suit in this behalf expended and the Defendant in mercy,
&c., But this Judgment may be discharged by payment of one hundred pounds in gold
and silver with Interest thereon to be computed after the rate of five percentum per
annum from the seventeenth day of July 1787 untill paid and the costs
    Plaintiff's costs   130 lbs tobacco @ 1 1/2   ]
                         75 lbs tobacco @ 1 1/4   ] p pounds & $ 8.38.
    Execution issued

p.   Hipkins v Mason
277   The Commonwealth of Virginia to the Sheriff of LOUDOUN County, Greeting
        We command you that you take ABRAHAM BARNES THOMPSON MASON

if he be found in your Bailiwick and him safely keep so that you have his body before the Judges of the District Court to be held at the Town of DUMFRIES at the next Court to answer LEWIS HIPKINS of a Plea of Debt for fifty five pounds, one shilling and one penny, damage thirty pounds, and have then there this Writ. Witness GEORGE BROOKE, Clerk of the Court at DUMFRIES the 30th day of July in the 15th year of the Commonwealth Ad. 1790

G. BROOKE   C. D. C.

Bond for payment of money.   CHARLES LEE for Plaintiff
Executed and STEPHEN THOMPSON MASON Appearance Bail

OSBORN KING, D. Sh.

FAIRFAX County to wit;

LEWIS HIPKINS complains of ABRAHAM BARNES THOMPSON MASON in custody and so forth of a Plea that he render to him the sum of fifty five pounds, one shilling and one penny current specie of Virginia which to him he owes and from him unjustly detains for this to wit, that whereas the Defendant on the fourteenth day of April in the year 1788 at the Parish of [blank] in the County aforesaid by his certain Writing Obligatory sealed with his seal and to the Court now here shewn the date whereof is on the same day and year as aforesaid, acknowledged himself to be held and firmly bound unto the Plaintiff in the sum of fifty five pounds, one shilling and one penny current specie of Virginia to be paid to him when required, Nevertheless the Defendant altho often required hath not paid to the Plaintiff the sum of fifty five pounds, one shilling and one penny but hath refused and still doth refuse to pay the same to him to his damage thirty pounds, and therefore he sues &c.

CHARLES LEE for Plaintiff

Pledges of prosecution, J. Doe & R. Roe	
November 1790	Declaration and Bond Common Order against Defendant and Security
December 1790	Common Order confirmed
May 1791	Special Bail, Common Order set aside & payment

KNOW ALL MEN by these presents that we ABRAHAM BARNES THOMPSON MASON and STEPHEN THOMPSON MASON of LOUDOUN County are held and

p.   Hipkins v Mason
278   firmly bound unto JAMES COLEMAN, Gent., Sheriff of the County, in the just and full sum of one hundred ten pounds, two shillings and two pence to the which payment well and truly to be made and done we bind ourselves and each of our heirs Executors and Administrators jointly and severally firmly by these presents; Sealed with our seals and dated this 21st day of September 1790

THE CONDITION of the above Obligation is such that if the above bound ABRAHAM BARNES THOMPSON MASON shall and do make his personal appearance before the Judges of the District Court to be held at the Town of DUMFRIES at the next Court to answer LEWIS HIPKINS of a Plea of Debt for fifty five pounds, one shilling and one penny, damage thirty pounds, that then the above Obligation to be void or else to remain in full force and virtue in Law

Sealed and delivered in presence of
OSBORN KING   ABRAHAM B. THOMSON MASON [seal]
                                 STEPHEN THOMSON MASON   [seal]
       KNOW ALL MEN by these presents that I ABRAHAM B. T. MASON of
LOUDOUN County and the State of Virginia am held and firmly bound unto LEWIS
HIPKINS of FAIRFAX County in the State of Virginia in the full and just sum of fifty
five pounds, one shilling and one penny current money of Virginia to be paid to LEWIS
HIPKINS his heirs Executors Administrators or assigns, to the which payment well
and truly to be made and done I bind myself my heirs Executors and Administrators
in and for the whole firmly by these presents, sealed with my seal and dated this
fourteenth day of April in the year of our Lord one thousand seven hundred and eighty
eight
       THE CONDITION of the above Obligation is such that if the above bound ABRA-
HAM B. T. MASON his heirs Executors and Administators do and shall pay or cause
to be paid unto LEWIS HIPKINS his heirs Executors Administrators or assigns the
full and just sum of twenty seven pounds, ten shillings and two pence half penny current specie of Virginia in gold coin at five pounds, six shillings and eight pence per
ounce, Spanish milled dollars at six shillings each and French Crown at six shillings
and eight pence each on demand, then the above Obligation to be void otherwise to
stand

p.   Hipkins v Mason
279   remain and be in full force power and virtue in Law
       Signed sealed and delivered in presence of
       THOMAS DARNE   AB: BARNES THOMSON MASON [seal]
October 17th 1793
       LEWIS HIPKINS, Plaintiff   ]
              against   ] In Debt
       ABRAHAM BARNES THOMPSON MASON, Defendant   ]
       This day came the parties by their Attornies and the Defendant relinquishing his
former Plea acknowledged the Plaintiff's action against him; therefore it is considered by the Court that the Plaintiff recover against the Defendant fifty five pounds,
one shilling and one penny current specie of Virginia, the Debt in the Declaration
mentioned, and his costs by him about his suit in this behalf expended, and the Defendant in mercy, &c., But this Judgment may be discharged by the payment of
twenty seven pounds, ten shillings and two pence current specie of Virginia in gold
coin at five pounds, six shillings and eight pence per ounce, Spanish milled dollars at
six shillings each and French Crowns at six shillings and eight pence each with
Interest thereon to be computed after the rate of five per centum per annum from
the fourteenth day of April 1788 untill paid and the costs
       Plaintiff's costs   100 lbs tobacco @ 1 1/2   ]
                             80 lbs tobacco @ 1 1/4   ] p pound & $ 7.92.
       Execution issued

Hartshorne v Littlejohn

The Commonwealth of Virginia to the Sheriff of LOUDOUN County Greeting. We command you that you take JOHN LITTLEJOHN if he be found within your Bailiwick and him safely keep so that you have his body before the Judges of the District Court to be held at the Town of DUMFRIES at the next Court to answer WILLIAM HARTSHORNE of a Plea of Debt for two hundred twenty eight pounds, fourteen shillings and two pence, damage ten pounds, and have then there this Writ. Witness GEORGE BROOKE, Clerk of the Court at DUMFRIES the 26th day of April in the fourteenth year of the Commonwealth A. D. 1790

G. BROOKE, C. D. D. C.

Debt due by Bond. Bail is required.   SIMMS for the Plaintiff
Came too late to hand to execute   OSBORN KING, D. Sh.

p.   ### Hartshorne v Littlejohn
280   The Commonwealth of Virginia to the Sheriff of LOUDOUN County, Greeting.
We command you that you take JOHN LITTLEJOHN if he be found within your Bailiwick and him safely keep so that you have his body before the Judges of the District Court at the Town of DUMFRIES at the next Court to answer WILLIAM HARTSHORNE of a Plea of Debt for two hundred twenty eight pounds, fourteen shillings and two pence, damage ten pounds, and have then there this Writ. Witness GEORGE BROOKE, Clerk of the Court at DUMFRIES this 24th day of July in the 15th year of the Commonwealth A. D. 1790

G. BROOKE   C. D. D. C.

For Debt due by Bond. Bail is required
Executed and JOHN WREN Appearance Bail
OSBORN KING, D Sh.

LOUDOUN County, to wit

WILLIAM HARTSHORNE complains of JOHN LITTLEJOHN in custody &c. of a Plea that he render unto him the sum of two hundred twenty eight pounds, fourteen shillings and two pence which to him he owes and from him unjustly detains for that whereas the Defendant on the 19th day of September in the year of our Lord one thousand seven hundred and eighty six at the Parish of [blank] and County aforesaid, by a certain Writing Obligatory sealed with his seal and to the Court now here shewn the date whereof is on the same day and year aforesaid did acknowledge himself to be held and firmly bound unto the Plaintiff in the sum of two hundred twenty eight pounds, fourteen shillings and two pence to be paid to the Plaintiff when the Defendant should be thereunto afterwards required, Nevertheless the Defendant altho often required the sum of money to the Plaintiff hath not paid but the same to him to pay hath altogether refused and still doth refuse to the damage of the Plaintiff [blank] pounds and therefore he brings suit &c.

SIMMS for the Plaintiff

Pledges &c. J. Doe & R. Roe
June 1790   Alias Capias
November 1790   Common Order against Defendant & Security
December 1790   Bail filed, Common Order confirmed
May 1791   Common Order set aside and payment

p. **Hartshorne v Littlejohn**
281   KNOW ALL MEN by these presents that we JOHN LITTLEJOHN and [blank] of the County of LOUDOUN are held and firmly bound unto JAMES COLEMAN, Gent., Sheriff of the County, in the full and just sum of four hundred fifty seven pounds, eight shillings and two pence, to which payment well and truly to be made and done we bind ourselves our and each of our heirs Executors and Administrators jointly and severally firmly by these presents, Sealed with our seals and dated this 12th day of August 1790

THE CONDITION of the above obligation is such that if the above bound JOHN LITTLEJOHN shall and do make his personal appearance before the Judges of the District Court to be held at the Town of DUMFRIES at the next Court to answer WILLIAM HARTSHORNE of a Plea of debt for two hundred twenty eight pounds, fourteen shillings and two pence, that then the above Obligation to be void or else to remain in full force and virtue

Sealed and delivered in presence of

    [no witnesses recorded]   JOHN LITTLEJOHN   [seal]
                              JOHN WREN   [seal]

LOUDOUN County Sct.

    Memorandum; That upon the 11th day of October in the year of our Lord 1790 SAMUEL DORSEY HARRYMAN of the County of LOUDOUN personally appeared before me, CHARLES BENNETT, one of the Justices of the County, and undertook for JOHN LITTLEJOHN at the suit of WILLIAM HARTSHORNE and COMPANY in an action of Debt now depending in the District Court held at DUMFRIES that in case JOHN LITTLEJOHN shall be cast in the suit he, JOHN LITTLEJOHN, will pay and satisfy the condemantion of the Court or render his body to Prison in Execution for the same or that he, SAMUEL DORSEY HARRIMAN, will do it for him; Acknowledged before me

                    CHAS: BENNETT

    KNOW ALL MEN by these presents that I JOHN LITTLEJOHN of LOUDOUN County and State of Virginia am held and firmly bound unto WILLIAM HARTSHORNE, Merchant of ALEXANDRIA, in the full and just sum of two hundred twenty eight pounds, fourteen shillings and two pence specie to be paid unto WILLIAM HARTSHORNE his certain Attorney Executors Administrators or assigns, to the which payment well and truly to be made and done, I bind myself my heirs Executors and Administrators firmly by these presents, Sealed with my

p. **Hartshorne v Littlejohn**
282   seal and dated the nineteenth day of September in the year of our Lord one thousand seven hundred and eighty six

THE CONDITION of the above Obligation is such tht if the above bound JOHN LITTLEJOHN do and shall well and truly pay or cause to be paid to WILLIAM HARTSHORNE or to his certain Attorney Executors Administrators or assigns the full and just sum of one hundred fourteen pounds, seven shillings and one penny specie in gold or silver at its passing value and that at or upon demand with Interest from March 16th last past for the same, then the above Obligation to be void else to remain in full force and virtue in Law

Sealed and delivered in presence of
    CHARLES SHOLL   JOHN LITTLEJOHN   [seal]
    HOSCA RENSHAW
October 17th 1793
    WILLIAM HARTSHORNE, Plaintiff   ]
          against   ] In Debt
    JOHN LITTLEJOHN, Defendant   ]

    This day came the parties by their Attornies and the Defendant relinquishing his former Plea acknowledged the Plaintiff's action against him; therefore it is considered by the Court that Plaintiff recover against the Defendant two hundred twenty eight pounds, fourteen shillings and two pence specie, the Debt in the Declaration mentioned, and his costs by him about his suit in this behalf expended, and the Defendant in mercy, &c., But this Judgment may be discharged by the payment of one hundred fourteen pounds, seven shillings and one penny in gold or silver with Interest thereon to be computed after the rate of five per centum per annum from the sixteenth day of March 1786 untill paid and the costs

    Plaintiff's costs   135 lbs tobacco @ 1 1/2]
                      95 lbs tobacco @ 1 1/4] p pound & $7.98.

    Execution issued

p.   Herbert & Potts v Carter's Admrs.
283   The Commonwealth of Virginia to the Sheriff of Prince William County, Greeting. We command you that you take LANDON CARTER, WORMLEY CARTER and ROBERT CARTER, Administrators of JOHN CARTER, deceased, if they be found within your Bailiwick and them safely keep so that you have their bodies before the Judges of the District Court at the next Court to be held at the Town of DUMFRIES to answer Messrs. HERBERT & POTTS, Assignees of CLEON MOORE of a Plea of Debt for fifty seven pounds, ten shillings current money of Virginia in specie, damage ten pounds, And then there have this Writ. Witness HUMPHREY BROOKE Clerk of the Court at DUMFRIES the 9th day of October in the 14th year of the Commonwealth A. D. 1789

                            H. BROOKE, C. D. D. C.
    An action for Debt due by Promissory Note being instituted against the Administrators. No Appearance Bill is to be required
                          J. LOVE for Plaintiffs
    Came to hand too late   GEORGE G. TAYLOR, D. Sh.

    The Commonwealth of Virginia to the Sheriff of Prince William County, Greeting; We command you as we have before commanded you that you take LANDON CARTER, WORMLEY CARTER and ROBERT CARTER, Administrators of JOHN CARTER, deceased, if they be found within your Bailiwick and them safely keep so that you have them before the Judges of the District Court to be held at the Town of DUMFRIES on the first day of next Court to answer Messrs. HERBERT & POTTS, Assignee of CLEON MOORE of a Plea of Debt for fifty seven pounds, ten shillings current money of Virginia in specie, damage ten pounds, And then there have

this Writ. Witness HUMPHREY BROOKE, Clerk of the Court at DUMFRIES the 19th day of October in the 14th year of the Commonwealth A. D. 1789
H. BROOKE, C. D. D. C.
On a Promissory Note, no Bail required
Executed on LANDON, WORMLEY and ROBERT CARTER
GEORGE GRAY TAYLOR, D. Sh.

p.   Herbert & Potts v Carter's Admrs.
284   LOUDOUN County, to wit;
WILLIAM HERBERT and JOHN POTTS, JUNR. Assignees of CLEON MOORE, complain of JOHN CARTER in custody &c. of a Plea that he render unto them fifty seven pounds, ten shillings current money of Virginia which to them he owes and from them unjustly detains for that whereas the Defendant on the 6th day of July in the year of our Lord 1787, at the Parish of [blank] and County aforesaid by his certain Writing Obligatory sealed with his seal and to the Court now here shewn, the date whereof is on the same day and year aforesaid, did acknowledge himself to be held and firmly bound to CLEON MOORE in the sum of fifty seven pounds, ten shillings current money of Virginia to be paid to CLEON MOORE when the Defendant should be thereunto afterwards required, and whereas afterwards, to wit on the [blank] day of July in the year of our Lord 1787, by his certain writing endorsed on the back of the Writing Obligatory with his proper hand and name thereto subscribed assigned the Writing Obligatory to the Plaintiffs of which Assignment the Defendant the day year and place last mentioned had notice by means whereof and by force of the Act of Assembly in such cases made and provided, action accrued to the Plaintiffs to demand and have of the Defendant the sum of fifty seven pounds, ten shillings current money of Virginia; Nevertheless the Defendant altho often required the sum of money to the Plaintiffs hath not paid but the same to them to pay hath altogether refused and still doth refuse to the damage of the Plaintiffs [blank] pounds therefore they bring suit, &c.

LOVE for the Plaintiffs

October 1789	Alias Capias
May 1790	Common Order against Defendants
August 1790	Continuance for Declaration
November 1790	ditto
December 1790	Declaration filed, Common Order confirmed
May 1791	Common Order set aside & payment

I JOHN CARTER of County of LOUDOUN do promise to pay to CLEON MOORE on order on or before the first day of December next the sum of fifty seven pounds, ten shillings current money of Virginia in specie at the

p.   Herbert & Potts v Carter's Admrs.
285   usual passing rates for a Negro man sold me named Frederick; As Witness my hand and seal this sixth day of July 1787
JOHN CARTER   [seal]
Pay the within to HERBERT & POTTS for value received
CLEON MOORE

October 17, 1793

HERBERT & POTTS, Assignees of CLEON MOORE, Plaintiffs]
    against] In Debt
LANDON CARTER, WORMLEY CARTER & ROBERT]
CARTER, Administrators of JOHN CARTER, deceased,]
Defendants]

This day came the parties by their Attornies and the Defendants relinquishing their former Plea acknowledged the action of the Plaintiffs against them; therefore it is considered by the Court that the Plaintiffs recover against the Defendants fifty seven pounds ten shillings current mney of Virginia, the Debt in the Declaration mentioned, and their costs by them about their suit in this behalf expended to be levied of the goods and chattles of the deceased at the time of his death in the hands of the Defendants to be administered if so much thereof in their hands they have but if not then the costs to be levied of their own proper good and chattles and the Defendants in mercy, &c.

Plaintiffs's costs   185 lbs tobacco @ 1 1/2]
                      70 lbs tobacco # 1 1/4] p pound & $7.98

Execution issued

Lyle's Exrs. v Dick

The Commonwealth of Virginia to the Sheriff of FAIRFAX County, Greeting. We command you that you take ELISHA C. DICK if he be found within your Bailiwick and him safely keep so that you have his body before the Judges of the District Court to be held at the Town of DUMFRIES at the next Court to answer WILLIAM HUNTER, JUNR., ANDREW WAILES, ROBERT LYLE and THOMAS HEWITT Executors of the Last Will and Testament of ROBERT LYLE, who was Assignee of MONICA CLIFFORD of a Plea of Debt for seventy six pounds, damage thirty pounds, and have then there this Writ. Witness GEORGE BROOKE, Clerk of the Court at DUMFRIES this 1st day of September in the 15th year of the Commonwealth A. D. 1791.

G. BROOKE, C. D. C.

p.   Lyle's Exrs. v Dick
286   For money due by Bond. CHARLES LEE for Plaintiffs
       Executed   BALDWIN DADE
FAIRFAX County, to wit

WILLIAM HUNTER, JUNR. ROBERT LYLE, ANDREW WAILES and THOMAS HEWITT, Executors of the Last Will and Testament of ROBERT LYLE, deceased, who was Assignee of MONICA CLIFFORD, complain of ELISHA C. DICK in custody, &c., of a Plea that he render to them the sum of seventy six pounds lawful money of Virginia which from them he unjustly detains for this, to wit, tht whereas the Defendant on the twenty first day of March in the year 1787 at the Parish of [blank] in the County aforesaid, by his certain Writing Obligatory sealed with his seal and to the Court here now shewn, the date whereof is on the same day and year aforesaid, acknowledged himself to be held and firmly bound unto MONICA CLIFFORD in the sum of seventy six pounds gold or silver money at the Virginia currency to be paid to MONICA CLIFFORD her certain Attorney, Executors Administrators or assigns when he should be required and whereas afterwards, to wit, on the 24th day of March in the year 1787, at the Parish and County aforesaid, MONICA CLIFFORD assigned the Writing [the same being then and there unpaid] unto ROBERT LYLE in his life time by endorseing the Assignment subscribed with her proper name and hand on the Writing whereof the Defendant then and there had notice, by virtue of which premises and of the Act of Assembly in such case made and provided, the Defendant became liable to pay to ROBERT LYLE in his life time and since his death to the Plaintiffs the sum of seventy six pounds when he should be required; Nevertheless the Defendant though often required hath not paid to ROBERT LYLE in his life time nor since his death to the Plaintiffs, his Executors, the sum of money but hath refused and still doth refuse to pay the same to their damage thirty pounds and therefore they sue &c. And they bring into Court Letters Testimentary whereby it sufficiently appears to the Court that they are the Executors of the Last Will and Testament of ROBERT LYLE and have thereof administration &c.

CHARLES LEE for Plaintiffs

Pledges of prosecution. John doe & R. Roe

p.   Lyle's Exrs. v Dick
287   November 1790   Bond & Declaration, Special Bail, Common Order
         December 1790   Common Order confirmed
         May 1791   Common Order set aside and payment

KNOW ALL MEN by these presents that I ELISHA C. DICK of FAIRFAX County and State of Virginia am held and firmly bound unto MONICA CLIFFORD of the County and State aforesaid in the full and just sum of seventy six pounds gold or silver money at the Virginia currency to be paid unto MONICA CLIFFORD her certain Attorney Executors Administrators or assigns to the which payment well and truly to be made and done, I bind myself my heirs Executors and Administrators and each of them firmly by these presents; Sealed with my seal and dated this 21st day of March in the year of our Lord one thosuand seven hundred and eighty seven

THE CONDITION of the above Obligation is such that if the above bound ELISHA C. DICK do and shall well and truly pay or cause to be paid unto MONICA CLIFFORD her certain Attorney, Executors Administrators or assigns the full and just sum of thirty eight pounds money aforesaid at or upon the first day of June with legal Interest for the same, then the above obligation to be void or else to remain in full force and virtue in Law

Sealed and deliverd in presence of
    JOHN DAGG   ELISHA C. DICK   [seal]
    JANE JOICE
I assign the within Bond to ROBERT LYLE received this 24th day of march 1787
Test W. ELLZEY   MONICA CLIFFORD

October 17th 1793
    WILLIAM HUNTER, JUNR. ANDREW WAILES, ROBERT   ]
    LYLE and THOMAS HEWITT, Executors of the Last Will and   ]

Testament of ROBERT LYLE, who was Assignee of MONICA]
CLIFFORD, Plaintiffs]
   against   ] In Debt
ELISHA C. DICK, Defendant]

This day came the parties by their Attornies and this suit abated as to the Plaintiff WILLIAM HUNTER, JUNR. by his death and threupon came also a Jury to wit

JAMES JOHNSON	HUGH FORBES	ADAM GARDENHIRE
JOHN PATTERSON	JOHN MAUZY	JAMES MITCHELL
JOHN LANGFITT	JOHN BROWN, SENR.	

p,
288   Lyle's Exrs. v Dick

                   JAMES HAYS
  SAMUEL TEBBS   THOMAS CHAPMAN and   JOHN BROWN, JUNR.

who being elected tried and sworn the truth to speak upon the issue joined upon their Oath do say that the Defendant hath not paid the debt in the Declaration mentioned as by replying the Plaintiffs have alledged and they do assess the Plaintiffs's damages by means of the detention of that debt to one penny besides their costs; therefore it is considered by the Court that the Plaintiffs recover against the Defendant seventy six pounds Virginia currency, the Debt in the Declaration mentioned, and the damages assessed and their costs by them about their suit in this behalf expended, and the Defendant in mercy, &c., But this Judgment may be discharged by the payment of thirty eight pounds current money aforesaid with Interest thereon to be computed after the rate of five per centum per annum from the twenty first day of March 1787 untill paid and the damages and costs

  Plaintiffs's costs   125 lbs tobacco @ 1 1/3   ]
           80 lbs tobacco @ 1 1/4   ] p pound & &10.23.
  Execution issued

    LYLE's Exrs. v Greenway
   The Commonwealth of Virginia to the Sheriff of FAIRFAX County, Greeting. We command you that you take JOSEPH GREENWAY if he be found within your Bailiwick and him safely keep so that you have his body before the Judges of the District Court to be held at the Town of DUMFRIES at the next Court to answer WILLIAM HUNTER, JUNR. ANDREW WAILES, ROBERT LYLE and THOMAS HEWITT, Executors of the Last Will and Testament of ROBERT LYLE, deceased of a Plea of Debt for thirty three pounds, eleven shillings and nine pence with legal Interest from the ninth day of March 1788, damage thirty pounds, and have then there this Writ. Witness GEORGE BROOKE, Clerk of the Court at DUMFRIES the 1st day of September in the 15th year of the Commonwealth A. D. 1790
            G. BROOKE, C. D. C.
   For Debt due by Bond. CHARLES LEE for Plaintiff
   Executed and JOHN FITZGERALD Appearance Bail
        p BALDWIN DADE
FAIRFAX County to wit;
   WILLIAM HUNTER, JUNR. ROBERT LYLE, ANDREW WAILES and THOMAS HEWITT, Executors of the Last Will and Testament of ROBERT LYLE,

deceased, complain

p.   Lyle's Exrs. v Greenway
289   of JOSEPH GREENWAY in custody and so forth that he render to them the
        sum of thirty three pounds, eleven shillings and nine pence with lawful Interest
from the 9th day of March 1788 which from them he unjustly detains for this, to wit,
tht whereas the Defendant on the ninth day of March in the year 1788 at the Parish
of [blank] and County aforesaid by his certain Writing Obligatory sealed with his seal
and to the Court now here shewn, the date whereof is on the same day and year
aforesaid; promised to pay to ROBERT LYLE in his life time the sum of thirty three
pounds, eleven shillings and nine pence lawful money of Virginia with Interest according to Law from the 9th day of March in the year 1788 when he should be required,
Nevertheless the Defendant tho often required hath not paid to ROBERT LYLE in his
life time or since his death to the Plaintiffs, his Executors, the sum of thirty three
pounds, eleven shillings and nine pence with Interest as aforesaid but hath refused
and still doth refuse to pay the same to them to their damage thirty pounds and
therefore they bring this suit, &c. and they also bring into Court Letters Testamentary whereby it appears that they are the Executors of the Last Will and Testament of ROBERT LYLE and have administration thereof &c.
                                        CHARLES LEE for Plaintiffs
        Pledges of prosecution, John Doe & R. Roe
        November 1790   Common Order against Defendant and Security
        December 1790   Common Order confirmed
        May 1791   Common Order set aside and payment

        KNOW ALL MEN by these presents that we JOSEPH GREENWAY and
JOHN FITZGERALD are held and firmly bound unto ROBERT TOWNSHEND
HOOE, Gent., Sheriff of FAIRFAX County, in the just and full sum of seventy pounds
current money of Virginia to be paid to ROBERT T. HOOE his Executors Administrators or assigns to which payment well and truly to be mde we bind ourselves and each
of us our and each of our heirs Executors and Administrators jointly and severally
firmly by these presents; Sealed with out seals and dated the 12th day of October
1790
        Whereas WILLIAM HUNTER, JUNR. ANDREW WAILES, ROBERT LYLE
and THOMAS

p   Lyle's Exrs. v Greenway
290   HEWITT, Executors of ROBERT LYLE, deceased, hath sued forth against
        JOSEPH GREENWAY out of the District Court at DUMFRIES a Writ of
capias ad respondendum in a Plea of Debt for thirty three pounds, eleven shillings and
nine pence, damage thirty pounds, directed to the Sheriff of the County of FAIRFAX
which hath been executed upon JOSEPH GREENWAY;
        Now the Condition of the above Obligation is such that if the above bound
JOSEPH GREENWAY do make his personal appearance at the next Court to be held
for the District at the Courthouse at DUMFRIES on the first day of October Court
and do then and there abide by fulfill and perform such Orders as by the Court shall
be made in the action and do not depart from the Court till the same shall be per-

formed then the above Obligation to be void or else to remain in full force power and virtue in Law

Signed and delivered in presence of

B. DADE   JOSEPH GREENWAY   [seal]
                                           JOHN FITZGERALD   [seal]

ALEXANDRIA, March 9th 1788

I promise to pay to ROBERT LYLE SENR. or order the sum of thirty three pounds, eleven shillings and nine pence current money with lawful Interest from this date till paid as witness my hand and seal

L. 33...11...9.   JOSEPH GREENWAY

April 12th 1788

Credit by Cash, L. 3.....0.....0.

At a District Court held at DUMFRIES the 17th of October 1793

WILLIAM HUNTER, JUNR. ANDREW WAILES, ROBERT   ]
LYLE and THOMAS HEWITT, Executors of ROBERT LYLE   ]
deceased, Plaintiffs   ]
        against   ] In Debt
JOSEPH GREENWAY, Defendant   ]

This day came the parties by their Attornies and the suit abates as to the Defendant, WILLIAM HUNTER, JUNR. by his death, and thereupon came also a Jury, to wit

JAMES JOHNSON	HUGH FORBES	ADAM GARDENHIRE
JOHN PATTERSON	JAMES HAYES	JOHN MAUZY
JOHN BROWN, SENR.	SAMUEL TEBBS	JAMES MITCHELL
THOMAS CHAPMAN	JOHN LANGFITT and	JOHN BROWN, JUNR.

who being elected tried and sworn the truth to speak upon the issue joined upon their Oath do say that the Defendant hath not paid the debt in the Declaration

p.   Lyle's Exrs. v Greenway
291   as by replying the Plaintiffs have alledged and they do assess the Plaintiffs's damage by means of the detention of that debt to five pounds, eight shillings besides their costs; therefore it is considered by the Court that the Plaintiffs recover against the Defendant the thirty three pounds, eleven shillings and nine pence with Interest thereon to be computed after the rate of five per centum per annum from the ninth day of March 1788 untill paid and their damages in form assessed and their costs by them about their suit in this behalf expended, and the Defendant in mercy, &c.

Plaintiffs's costs   100 lbs tobacco @ 1 1/2   ]
                       70 lbs tobacco @ 1 1/4   ] p pound & $10.23
Execution issued

Lewis & Bingham v Daw

The Commonwealth of Virginia to the Sheriff of LOUDOUN County, Greeting. We command you that you take PETER DAW if he be found within your Bailiwick and him safely keep so that you have his body before the Judges of the District Court to be held at the Town of DUMFRIES at the next Court to answer MORDECAI

LEWIS and WILLIAM BINGHAM, Assignees of WILLIAM HARTSHORNE, who was Assignee of GURDEN CHAPIN & COMPANY, of a Plea of Debt for seventy pounds, thirteen shillings and four pence, damage ten pound, and have then there this Writ. Witnes GEORGE BROOKE, Clerk of the Court at DUMFRIES the tenth day of April in the 14th year of the Commonwealth A. D. 1790

G. BROOKE, C. D. D.. C.

For Debt due by Penal Bill. Bond is required   SIMMS
Came too late to hand to execute p

JAMES JENKINS, D. S.

The Commonwealth of Virginia to the Sheriff of LOUDOUN County, Greeting. We command you as we have at another time commanded you that you take PETER DAW if he be found within your Bailiwick and him safely keep so that you have his body before the Judges of the District Court to be held at the Town of DUMFRIES at the next Court to answer MORDECAI LEWIS & WILLIAM BINGHAM, Assignees of WILLIAM HARTSHORNE, who was Assignee of GURDEN CHAPIN and

p.   Lewis & Bingham v Daw
292   COMPANY of a Plea of Debt for seventy pounds, thirteen shillings and four
        pence, damage ten pounds, and have then there this Writ. Witness GEORGE
BROOKE, Clerk of the Court at DUMFRIES the 26th day of July in the 15th year of the Commonwealth, A. D. 1790

G. BROOKE, D. C. C. D.

For Debt due by Penal Bill. Bail is required
Executed and WILLIAM HICKMAN Appearance Bail

WILLIAM R. TAYLOR, D. S.

LOUDOUN County, to wit

MORDECAI LEWIS and WILLIAM BINGHAM, Assignees of WILLIAM HARTSHORNE who was Assignee of GURDEN CHAPIN & COMPANY, complain of PETER DAW in custody, &c., of a Plea that he render unto them the just and full sum of seventy pounds, thirteen shillings and four pence which to them he owes and from them unjustly detains for that whereas the Defendant on the 21st day of March 1788 at the Parish of [blank] and County aforesaid, by his certain Bill Obligatory sealed with his seal and to the Court now here shewn, whose date is on the same day and year did promise to pay to GURDEN CHAPIN & COMPANY or order on demand thirty five pounds, six shillings and eight pence with lawful Interest for the same in silver dollars at six shillings each or other gold or silver in proportion for value received to which payment he bound himself his heirs Executors and Administrators in the penal sum of seventy pounds, thirteen shillings and four pence like money as above and the Plaintiffs in fact say that the Defendant did not pay to GURDEN CHAPIN & COMPANY or either of them the sum of thirty five pounds, six shillings and eight pence with lawful Interest when required to wit on the [blank] day of [blank] 17[blank] at the Parish and County aforesaid which he ought to have paid according to the form and effect of the Bill Obligatory whereby an action accrued to GURDEN CHAPIN & COMPANY to demand and have of the Defendant the sum of seventy pounds, thirteen shillings and four pence; And whereas GURDEN CHAPIN & COMPANY

p.   Lewis & Bingham v Daw
293   afterwards, to wit, on the sixteenth day of February 1790 at the Parish and
        County aforesaid, the sum of seventy pounds, thirteen shillings and four pence
and every penny thereof being then and there due and unpaid by their certain Writing
endorsed on the back of the Bill with their proper hands and names thereto subscribed assigned the Bill Obligatory to WILLIAM HARTSHORNE, by means whereof
WILLIAM became entitled to receive the sum of seventy pounds, thirteen shillings
and four pence, the penalty of the Bill, and the same being so due and unpaid,
WILLIAM afterwards, to wit, on the 5th day of April 1790 at the Parish and County
aforesaid by his certain writing endorsed on the back of the Bill with his proper hand
and name thereto subscribed assigned the Bill to MORDECAI LEWIS & COMPANY,
which Company consists of MORDECAI LEWIS & WILLIAM BINGHAM, for value
received of which several Assignments the Defendant the day year and place last
mentioned had notice by virtue whereof and by force of the Act of Assembly in that
case made and provided, action accrued to the Plaintiffs to demand and have of the
Defendant the sum of seventy pounds, thirteen shillings and four pence, yet the Defendant altho often required the sum of money last mentioned or any penny thereof
unto the Plaintiffs or to either of them hath not paid but the same to pay hath altogether refused and still doth refuse to the damage of the Plaintiffs [blank] pounds and
therefore they bring suit &c.

                        SIMMS for the Plaintiffs

        Pledges &c. J. Doe & R. Roe
        June 1790   Alias Capias
        November 1790   Common Order against Defendant & Security
        December 1790   Common Order confirmed
        May 1791   Common Order set aside and payment

p.   Lewis & Bingham v Daw
294   LOUDOUN County, to wit
        Memorandum; That on the sixth day of May in the year of our Lord one thou-
sand seven hundred and ninety one SAMUEL CANBY of the County of LOUDOUN
personally appeared before me, JOHN ALEXANDER, Gentleman, one of the Justices
of the Peace for the County, and undertook for PETER DAW at the suit of WILLIAM
BINGHAM and MORDECAI LEWIS, Assignees of WILLIAM HARTSHORNE and
CO., in an action of Debt now depending in the District Court of DUMFRIES that in
case PETER DAW shall be cast in the suit he will satisfy and pay the condemnation
of the Court or render his body to Prison in Execution for the same or tht he,
SAMUEL CANBY, will do it for him. Acknowledged before me
                        JNO: ALEXANDER
        I promise to pay to GURDEN CHAPIN & COMPANY or order on demand the
sum of thirty five pounds, six shillings and eight pence with lawful Interest for the
same in silver dollars at six shillings each or other silver or gold in proportion for value
received to which payment I bind myself my heirs Executors and Administrators in
the penal sum of seventy pounds, thirteen shillings and four pence like money; Witness my hand and seal this twenty first day of March in the year one thousand seven
hundred and eighty eight
Sealed and delivered in the presence of

AQUILA BROWNE   PETER DAW
Pay the within to Mr. WILLIAM HARTSHORNE
                                        GURDEN CHAPIN & CO
                                        February 16th 1790
        I assign the within Note to MORDECAI LEWIS & CO. for value received,
April 5th 1790.   WILLIAM HARTSHORNE
October 17th 1793
        MORDECAI LEWIS & WILLIAM BINGHAM, Assignees of   ]
        WILLIAM HARTSHORNE, who was Assignee of GURDEN   ]
        CHAPIN & COMPANY, Plaintiffs   ]
                        against   ] In Debt
        PETER DAW

p.   Lewis & Bingham v Daw
295   This day came the parties by their Attornies and the Defendant relinquishing
        his former Plea acknowledged the Plaintiffs's action against him; therefore it is
considered by the Court that the Plaintiffs recover against the Defendant seventy
pounds, thirteen shillings and four pence in silver dollars at six shillings each or other
silver or gold in proportion, the Debt in the Declaration mentioned, and their costs by
them about their suit in this behalf expended, and the Defendant in mercy &c. But
this Judgment may be discharged by the payment of thirty five pounds, six shillings
and eight pence like money with Interest thereon to be computed after the rate of five
per centum per annum from the twenty first day of March 1788 untill paid and the
costs
        Plaintiffs's costs   135 lbs tobacco @ 1 1/2   ]
                                95 lbs tobacco @ 1 1/4   ] p pound & $8.38
        Execution issued

        Lewis & Bingham v Hough
        The Commonwealth of Virginia to the Sheriff of LOUDOUN County, Greeting.
We command you that you take SAMUEL HOUGH if he be found within your Baili-
wick and him safely keep so that you have his body before the Judges of the District
Court to be held at the Town of DUMFRIES at the next Court to answer MORDE-
CAI LEWIS and WILLIAM BINGHAM, Assignees of WILLIAM HARTSHORNE &
COMPANY of a Plea of Debt for forty pounds, eighteen shillings and six pence,
damage ten pounds; And have then there this Writ. Witness GEORGE BROOKE,
Clerk of the Court at DUMFRIES the 10th day of April in the 14th year of the Com-
monwealth A. D. 1790
                                        G. BROOKE, C. D. D. C.
        For Debt due by Penal Bill. Bail is required
                                        SIMMS
        Came too late to hand to execute
                                        OSBORN KING, D. Sh.

        The Commonwealth of Virginia to the Sheriff of LOUDOUN County Greeting.
We command you as we have at another time commanded you that you ake
SAMUEL HOUGH if he be found within your Bailiwick

p.   **Lewis & Bingham v Hough**
296   and him safely keep so that you have his body before the Judges of the
District Court to be held at the Town of DUMFRIES at the next Court to
answer MORDECAI LEWIS and WILLIAM BINGHAM, Assigness of WILLIAM
HARTSHORNE & COMPANY of a Plea of Debt for forty pounds, eighteen shillings
and six pence, damage ten pounds, and have then there this Writ. Witness GEORGE
BROOKE, Clerk of the Court at DUMFRIES this 24th day of July in the 15th year of
the Commonwealth A. D. 1790

                G. BROOKE, C. D. D. C.

    For Debt due by Penal Bill. Bail is required
LOUDOUN County, to wit
    MORDECAI LEWIS & WILLIAM BINGHAM, Assigness of WILLIAM
HARTSHORNE & COMPANY complain of SAMUEL HOUGH in custody &c. of a
Plea that he render unto them the just and full sum of forty pounds, eighteen shillings
and six pence specie which he owes and from them unjustly detains for that whereas
the Defendant on the twenty fifth day of April in the year one thousand seven hundred and eighty six at the Parish of [blank] and County aforesaid by his certain Bill
Obligatory sealed with his seal and to the Court now here shewn the date whereof is
on the same day and year aforesaid, did promise to pay to WILLIAM HARTS-
HORNE or order on demand the sum of twenty pounds, nine shillings and three pence
specie in dollars at six shillings each or other silver or gold in proportion for value received to the payment well and truly to be made he bound himself his heirs Executors
and Administrators in the penal sum of forty pounds, eighteen shillings and six pence
like money as above and the Plaintiffs in fact say that the Defendant did not pay unto
WILLIAM HARTSHORNE & COMPANY or to either of them the sum of twenty
pounds, nine shillings and three pence or any penny thereof when required to wit, on
the [blank] day of [blank] in the year 17[blank] at the Parish and County aforesaid which
ought to have been paid according to the form and effect of the Bill Obligatory whereby an action accrued to WILLIAM HARTSHORNE & COMPANY to demand

p.   **Lewis & Bingham v Hough**
297   and have of the Defendant the sum of forty pounds, eighteen shillings and six
        pence and whereas WILLIAM HARTSHORNE & COMPANY afterwards, to
wit, the fifth day of April in the year one thousand seven hundred and ninety at the
Parish and County aforesaid the sum of forty pounds, eighteen shillings and six pence
and every penny thereof being then and there due and unpaid assigned the Bill Obligatory to MORDECAI LEWIS & COMPANY for value received which Company consists of MORDECAI LEWIS & WILLIAM BINGHAM by his writing endorsed on the
back of the Bill Obligatory signed with his proper hand and name of WILLIAM
HARTSHORNE for WILLIAM HARTSHORNE & COMPANY of which Assignment
the Defendant the day, year and place last mentioned had notice by means whereof
and by force of the Act of Assembly in such cases made and provided acton accrued
to the Plaintiffs to demand and have of the Defendant the sum of forty pounds, eighteen shillings and six pence, yet the Defendant altho often required the last mentioned
sum of money or any penny thereof hath not paid to the Plaintiffs or either of them
but the same to them hath altogether refused and still doth refuse to pay to the
damage of the Plaintiffs [blank] pounds therefore they bring suit &c.

SIMMS for the Plaintiffs

Pledges &c. J. Doe & R. Roe
June 1790   Alias Capias
November 1790   Common Order against Defendant & Security
December 1790   Common Order confirmed
May 1791   Common Order set aside and payment by Security

KNOW ALL MEN by these presents that we SAMUEL HOUGH and
WILLIAM STABLER of LOUDOUN County are held and firmly bound unto JAMES
COLEMAN, Gent., Sheriff of the County, in the full and just sum of eighty one
pounds, seventeen shillings to which payment well and truly to be made we bind ourselves our and each of our Executors and Administrators jointly and severally firmly
by these presents; sealed with our seal and dated this 21st day of September 1790

p.   Lewis & Bingham v Hough
298   THE CONDITION of the above Obligation is such that if the above bound
         SAMUEL HOUGH shall and do make his personal appearance before the
Judges of the District Court to be held at the Town of DUMFRIES at the next Court
to answer MORDECAI LEWIS & WILLIAM BINGHAM, Assignees of WILLIAM
HARTSHORNE & COMPANY of a Plea of Debt for forty pounds, eighteen shillings
and six pence, damage ten pounds, tht then the above Obligation to be void or else to
remain in full force and virtue
Sealed and delivered in presence of
         OSBORN KING   SAMUEL HOUGH   [seal]
                                          WM: STABLER   [seal]
         I promise to pay WILLIAM HARTSHORNE & CO. or order on demand the
sum of twenty pounds, nine shillings and three pence specie in dollars at six shillings
each or other silver or gold in proportion for value received, to which payment I bind
myself my heirs Executors and Administrators in the penal sum of forty pounds,
eighteen shillings and six pence like money as above. Witness my hand and seal this
twenty fifth day of April in the year one thousand seven hundred and eighty six
Sealed and delivered in presence of
         JNO: BEALLE   SAMUEL HOUGH
         I assign the within Note to MORDECAI LEWIS & CO. for value received
April 5th 1790   WILLIAM HARTSHORNE for
                                          WILLIAM HARTSHORNE & CO.

October 17th 1793
         MORDECAI LEWIS & WILLIAM BINGHAM, Assignees of   ]
         WILLIAM HARTSHORNE & CO., Plaintiffs   ]
                  against   ] In Debt
         SAMUEL HOUGH, Defendant   ]
    This day came the parties by their Attornies and the Defendant relinquishing his
former Plea acknowledged the Plaintiffs's action against him; therefore it is considered by the Court that the Plaintiffs recover against the Defendant and WILLIAM
STABLER, his Security, forty pounds, eighteen shillings and six pence in dollars at six
shillings each or other gold or silver in proportion, the Debt in the Declaration mentioned and their costs by them about their suit in this behalf expended, and the De-

fendant in mercy, &c. But this Judgment may be discharged by payment of twenty pounds, nine shillings and three pence like money with Interest thereon to be computed after the rate of five per centum per annum from the 25th day of April 1786 untill paid and the costs

Plaintiffs's costs   135 lbs tobacco @ 1 1/2]
                 95 lbs tobacco @ 1 1/4] p pounds & $ 8.38.

p.   West's Exr. v Scolefield & Lacey
299   The Commonwealth of Virginia to the Sheriff of LOUDOUN County, Greeting We command you that you take THOMAS SCOLEFIELD and JOSEPH LACEY if they be found within your Bailiwick and them safely keep so that you have their bodies before the Judges of the District Court to be held at the Town of DUMFRIES at the next Court to answer JOHN TYLER, Executor of CHARLES WEST, of a Plea of Debt for one hundred ten pounds specie, damage ten pounds, And have then there this Writ. Witness GEORGE BROOKE, Clerk of the Court at DUMFRIES the third day of March in the 14th year of the Commonwealth A. D. 1790

G. BROOKE, C. D. D. C.

Due by Bond.
Executed on both the within mentioned, JOHN MOORE   Appearance Bail
                 F. ADAMS, D. S. L. C.

May 1790	Special Bail
June 1790	Common Order
August 1790	Continued for Declaration
November 1790	do
December 1790	Declaration filed, Common Order confirmed
May 1791	Common Order set aside and payment

LOUDOUN County, to wit
JOHN TYLER, Executor of the Last Will and Testament of CHARLES WEST, deceased, complains of THOMAS SCOLEFIELD and JOSEPH LACEY in custody & so forth of a Plea that they render unto him the sum of one hundred ten pounds specie which from him they unjustly detain for that whereas the Defendants on the 19th day of September in the year of our Lord one thousand seven hundred and eighty three at the Parish of Shelburne and County aforesaid by their certain Writing Obligatory sealed with the seals of the Defendants and to the Court here shewn, the date whereof is the same day and year acknowledged themselves to be held and firmly bound unto CHARLES WEST in his life time in the sum of one hundred ten pounds specie to be paid to CHARLES WEST whenever after they should be

p.   West's Exr. v Scolefield & Lacey
300   required, Nevertheless the Defendants although often afterwards required to wit at the day and year aforesaid at the Parish and County aforesaid the sum of one hundred ten pounds specie to CHARLES WEST in his life time or to the Plaintiff after the death of CHARLES WEST or to either of them have not yet paid but the Defendant has hitherto entirely refused to pay the sum of money to the CHARLES WEST in his life time or to the Plaintiff after the decease of CHARLES WEST and

and still refuse to pay the same to the damage of the Plaintiff [blank] pounds and therefore he brings suit, &c., And the Plaintiff brings here into Court his Letters Testamentary by which it sufficiently appears to the Court here that the Plaintiff is Executor thereof and so forth

S. T. MASON, for Plaintiff

Pledges &c. John Doe & Richd. Roe

KNOW ALL MEN by these presents that we THOMAS SCOLEFIELD, JOSEPH LACEY and JOHN MOORE of County of LOUDOUN are held and firmly bound unto JAMES COLEMAN, Sheriff of the County, in the full and just sum of two hundred twenty pounds specie, to which payment well and truly to be made and done we bind ourselves our and each of our heirs Executors and Administrators jointly and severally firmly by these presents; Sealed with our seals and dated this 30th day of April 1790

THE CONDITION of the above Obligation is such that if the above bound THOMAS SCOLEFIELD and JOSEPH LACEY shall and do make their personal appearace before the Judges of the District Court to be held at the Town of DUMFRIES on the first day of the next Court to answer JOHN TYLER, Executor of CHARLES WEST, deceased, of a Plea of Debt for one hundred ten pounds specie as aforesaid, damage ten pounds, that then this Obligation to be void or else to remain in full force and virtue in Law

Sealed and delivered in presence of

F. ADAMS, D. S.

THOMAS SCOLEFIELD	[seal]
JOSEPH LACEY	[seal]
JOHN MOORE	[seal]

KNOW ALL MEN by these presents that we THOMAS SCOLEFIELD and JOSEPH LACEY are held and firmly bound unto CHARLES WEST of LOUDOUN County in the full sum of one hundred ten pounds specie to be paid to

p. West's Exr. v Scolefield & Lacey

301 CHARLES WEST his certain Attorney his heirs &c., to which payment well and truly to be made we bind ourselves our heirs Executors and Administrators jointly and severally firmly by these presents; Sealed with our seals and dated the 19th day of September 1783.

THE CONDITION of the above Obligation is such that if the above bound THOMAS SCOLEFIELD and JOSEPH LACEY do well and truly pay to CHARLES WEST his heirs or assigns the sum of fifty five pounds current money in half Joanners at forty eight shillings each on or before the first day of October in the year of our Lord one thousand seven hundred and eighty seven, then the above Obligation to be void or else to remain in force

Sealed & delivered in presence of

P. BAYLY

CHARLES WEST, JUNR.

December 7th 1789.

THOMAS SCOLEFIELD	[seal]
JOSEPH LACEY	[seal]

By Cash of THOMAS SCOLEFIELD six pounds and four pence for the Interest on the within Bond to the date above

JNO: TYLER

October 17th 1793

JOHN TYLER, Executor of CHARLES WEST, Plaintiff   ]
        against   ] In Debt
THOMAS SCOLEFIELD & JOSEPH LACEY, Defendants]

This day came the parties by their Attornies and the Defendants relinquishing their former Plea acknowledged the Plaintiff's action against them; therefore it is considered by the Court that Plaintiff recover against the Defendants one hundred ten pounds specie, the Debt in the Declaration mentioned, and their costs by them about their suit in this behalf expended, and the Defendant in mercy, &c. But this Judgment is to be discharged by the payment of fifty five pounds like money with Interest thereon to be computed after the rate of five per centum per annum from the first day of October 1788 untill paid and the costs

Plaintiff's costs   140 lbs tobacco @ 1 1/2   ]
                    70 lbs tobacco @ 1 1/4   ] p pound & $7.38

Execution issued

p.   West's Exr. v Scolefield & Lacey
302   The Commonwealth of Virginia to the Sheriff of LOUDOUN County, Greeting
We command you to take THOMAS SCOLEFIELD and JOSEPH LACEY if they be found in your Bailiwick and them safely keep so that you have them before the Judges of the District Court to be held at the Town of DUMFRIES at the next Court to answer JOHN TYLER, Executor of CHARLES WEST, of a Plea of Debt for one hundred ten pounds specie, damage ten pounds, And have then there this Writ. Witness GEORGE BROOKE, Clerk of the Court at DUMFRIES this third day of March in the 14th year of the Commonwealth A. D. 1790

                                 G. BROOKE, C. D. D. C.
Due by Bond
Executed on both the within mentioned, JOHN MOORE Appearance Bail
                        F. ADAMS, D. S. L. C.

May 1790	Special Bail
June 1790	Common Order
August 1790	Continuance for Declaration
November 1790	ditto
December 1790	Declcartion filed, Common Order confirmed
May 1791	Common Order set aside and payment

LOUDOUN County, to wit

JOHN TYLER, Executor of the Last Will and Testament of CHARLES WEST deceased, complains of THOMAS SCOLFIELD and JOSEPH LACEY in custody and so forth of a Plea that they render unto him the sum of one hundred ten pounds specie which from him they unjustly detain for that whereas the Defendants on the nineteenth day of September in the year of our Lord one thousand seven hundred and eighty three at the Parish of Shelburne and County aforesaid by their certain Writing Obligatory sealed with the seals of the Defendants and to this Court now here shewn the date whereof is the same day and year, acknowledged themselves to be held and firmly bound unto CHARLES WEST in his life time in the sum of one hundred ten pounds specie to be paid to CHARLES WEST whenever after they should be thereunto required, Nevertheless the Defendants altho often afterwards required to wit at the day and eyar aforesaid at the Parish and County aforesaid the

p. West's Exr. v Scolefield & Lacey
303 sum of one hundred ten pounds specie to CHARLES WEST in his life time or to the Plaintiff after the decease of CHARLES WEST or either of them have not yet paid but the Defendants have hitherto refused to pay the sum of money to CHARLES WEST in his life time or to the Plaintiff after the decease of CHARLES WEST, and still refuse to pay to the damage of the Plaintiff [blank] pounds and therefore he brings suit and so forth, And the Plaintiff brings here into Court his Letters Testamentary by which it sufficiently appears to the Court that the Plaintiff is Executor of the Last Will and Testament of CHARLES WEST, deceased, and has the Execution and so forth

S. T. MASON for Plaintiff

Pledges of Prosecution, Jno Doe & Richd. Roe

KNOW ALL MEN by these presents that we THOMAS SCOLFIELD, JOSEPH LACEY and JOHN MOORE of the County of LOUDOUN are held and firmly bound unto JAMES COLEMAN, Sheriff of the County, in the full and just sum of two hundred twenty pounds specie, to which payment well and truly to be made and done we bind ourselves and each of our heirs Executors and Administrators jointly and severally firmly by these presents; Sealed with our seals and dated the 30th day of April 1790

THE CONDITION of the above Obligation is such that if the above bound THOMAS SCOLFIELD and JOSEPH LACEY shall and do make their personal appearance before the Judges of the District Court to be held at the Town of DUMFRIES at the next Court to answer JOHN TYLER, Executor of CHARLES WEST, deceased, of a Plea of Debt for one hundred ten pounds specie as aforesaid, damage ten pounds, that then the above Obligation to be void or else to remain in full force and virtue

Sealed and delivered in presence of

F. ADAMS, D. S.　　　　THOMAS SCHOLFIELD [seal]
　　　　　　　　　　　　JOSEPH LACEY　　[seal]
　　　　　　　　　　　　JOHN MOORE　　　[seal]

KNOW ALL MEN by these presents that we THOMAS SCOLFIELD and JOSEPH LACEY are held and firmly bound unto CHARLES WEST of LOUDOUN County

p. West's Exr. v Scolfield & Lacey
304 in the sum of one hundred ten pounds specie to be paid to CHARLES WEST his certain Attorney his heirs Executors and Administrators to which payment we bind ourselves our heirs Executors and Administrators jointly and severally firmly by these presents; Sealed with our seals and dated this 19th day fo September 1783

THE CONDITION of the above Obligation is such that if the above bound THOMAS SCOLFIELD and JOSEPH LACEY their heirs Executors and Administrators shall well and truly pay to CHARLES WEST his heirs or assigns the full sum of fifty five pounds like money on or before the first day of October in the year of our Lord one thousand seven hundred and eighty nine without fraud or further delay, then the

above Obligation to be void else to remain in full force and virtue
Sealed and delivered in the presence of

P. BAYLY	THOMAS SCOLFIELD	[seal]
CHARLES WEST, JUNR	JOSEPH LACEY	[seal]

December 7th 1789., By Cash of THOMAS SCOLFIELD six pounds and four
pence for the Interest on the within Bond to the date above.

JNO: TYLER

October 17th 1793

JOHN TYLER, Executor of CHARLES WEST, deceased Plaintiff]
          against   ] In Debt
THOMAS SCHOLFIELD and JOSEPH LACEY, Defendants   ]

This day came the parties by their Attornies and the Defendants relinquishing
their former Plea acknowledged the Plaintiff's action against them; therefore it is
considered by the Court that the Plaintiff recover against the Defendants one hundred ten pounds specie, the Debt in the Declaration mentioned, and his costs by him
in this behalf expended and the Defendants in mercy, &c. But this Judgment may be
discharged by the payment of fifty five pounds like money with Interest thereon to be
computed after the rate of five per centum per annum from the first day of October
1788 untill paid and the costs

Plaintiff's costs	140 lbs tobacco @ 1 1/2	]
	70 lbs tobacco @ 1 1/4	] p pound & $7.38
Execution issued		

p.
305   [The next suit on pages 305 through 307, is identical to the two previous suits which are
306   identical, JOHN TYLER, Executor of CHARLES WEST, deceased, against THOMAS
307   SCHOLFIELD and JOSEPH LACEY]

p.   <u>Mills's Admr. v Chilton & Blackwell</u>
307   The Commonwealth of Virginia to the Sheriff of FAUQUIER County,
       Greeting; We command you as we have at another time commanded you to
take CHARLES CHILTON and JOSEPH BLACKWELL if they be found within your
Bailiwick and them safely keep so that you have them before the Judges of the
District Court to be held at the Town of DUMFRIES at the next Court to answer
ROBERT TOWSHEND HOOE, WILLIAM BROWN and CHARLES SIMMS,
Administrators &c. of JOHN MILLS, deceased, of a Plea of Debt for twelve thousand
pounds of crop tobacco and fifty shillings or five hundred pounds of tobacco, damage
ten pounds, And have then there this Writ. Witness GEORGE BROOKE, Clerk of
the Court at DUMFRIES the 24th day of November in the 15th year of the Commonwealth A. D. 1790

G. BROOKE, C. D. C.

p.   <u>Mills's Admrs. v Chilton & Blackwell</u>
308   For Debt due by Judgment, Bail is required

Executed on the within CHARLES CHILTON and JOSEPH BLACKWELL and CHARLES MARSHALL, Security
by AUGUSTINE JENNINGS, D. S.

FAUQUIER County, to wit

ROBERT TOWNSHEND HOOE, WILLIAM BROWN and CHARLES SIMMS Administrators of all and singular the goods and chattles rights and credits of JOHN MILLS, deceased, complain against CHARLES CHILTON and JOSEPH BLACK-WELL, Deputy Sheriff of FAUQUIER County in custody, &c. of a Plea that they render unto them the just and full quantity of four thousand fifteen poounds of crop tobacco with legal Interest thereon from the 28th of June 1784 and also the further quantity of four hundred ninety five pounds of gross tobacco and fifty shillings current money of Virignia which to them they owe and from them unjustly detain for that whereas the Plaintiffs at a General Court held for the Commonwealth of Virginia in October 1786, by the Judgment of the Court did recover against the Defendants the quantity of twelve thousand pounds of crop tobacco and costs; but to be discharged by the payment of four thousand one hundred fifteen pounds of crop tobacco inspected at some Warehouse on the POTOMACK RIVER above AQUIA WAREHOUSE, with five per cent interest thereon from the 28th day of June 1784 till payment and the costs which in addition to the costs of April 1786 amount the quantity of four hundred ninety five pounds gross tobacco and fifty shillings as by the Record thereof in the same Court remaining more fully is manifest and appears which Judgment yet remains in its full force and effect not satisfied or reversed and the Plaintiffs and the Plaintiffs have not yet sued out their Execution on the Judgment in form recovered whereby an action to the Plaintiffs has accrued to demand and have of the Defendants the four thousand one hundred fifteen pounds of crop tobacco with Interest together with the four hundred ninety five pounds gross tobacco and fifty shillings for their costs and charges by them about their suit in that particular expressed yet the

p.   Mills's Admrs. v Chilton & Blackwell
309   Defendants altho thereto often required the four thousand one hundred fifty pounds of crop tobacco with Interest and any part thereof or the four hundred ninety five pounds of gross tobacco with the fifty shillings or any part thereof to the Plaintiffs or either of them have not nor hath either of them paid but the same to them to pay they have altogether refued and still do refuse to the damage of the Plaintiffs [blank] pounds, therefore they bring their suit, &c.
SIMMS for the Plaintiffs

Pledges &c. J. Doe & R. Roe		
November 1790	Alias Capias	
December 1790	Declaration filed	
May 1791		[Bail filed abates against CHILTON
June 1791	Common Order	[Common Order against BLACKWELL
	& Iinquiry	[and Security

KNOW ALL MEN by these presents that we CHARLES CHILTON, JOSEPH BLACKWELL and CHARLES MARSHALL are held and firmly bound unto THO-MAS BRONAUGH, Gent., Sheriff of FAUQUIER County, in the just and full quantity of twenty four thousand pounds of crop tobacco and fourteen pounds, eleven shillings and ten pence half penny current money of Virginia to be paid unto THOMAS BRO-

NAUGH his heirs Executors Administrators or assigns to which payment well and
truly to be made and done we bind ourselves and each of our heirs Executors and
Administrators jointly and severally firmly by these presents; Sealed with our seals
and dated this [blank] day of February 1791

THE CONDITION of the above Obligation is such that if the above bound
CHARLES CHILTON and JOSEPH BLACKWELL shall make their personal appearance at the next District Court to be held at the Town of DUMFRIES then and
there to answer the suit of ROBERT TOWNSHEND DADE, WILLIAM BROWN
and CHARLES SIMMS, Administrators &c. of JOHN MILLS, deceased, of a Plea of
Debt for twelve thousand pounds of crop tobacco and four hundred ninety five pounds
of gross tobacco and fifty shillings or five hundred pounds of tobacco, damage ten
pounds, then the above Obligation to be void and of no effect otherwise to remain in
full force power and virtue

p.   Mills's Admrs. v Chilton & Blackwell
310   Signed sealed and delivered in the presence of
                AUGUSTINE JENNINGS, D. S.   CHARLES CHILTON   [seal]
                                               JOSEPH BLACKWELL   [seal]
                                               CHARLES MARSHAL   [seal]

Virginia   October General Court 1786.
        ROBERT TOWNSHEND HOOE, WILLIAM BROWN &   ]
        CHARLES SIMMS, Administrators &c. of JOHN MILLS,   ]
        deceased, Plaintiffs   ]
                against   ]   In Case
        CHARLES CHILTON, Defendant   ]
    Judgment for the Plaintiffs against the Defendant and JOSEPH BLACKWELL,
Deputy Sheriff of FAUQUIER County for twelve thousand pounds of crop tobacco
and costs, but to be discharged by the payment of four thousand one hundred fifteen
poounds of crop tobacco inspected at some Warehouses on POTOMACK RIVER
above AQUIA WAREHOUSE with five per cent Interest from the 28th day of June
1784 till payment and the costs,
            Costs in addition to the Judgment of April 1786, 190 lbs gross tobacco
                        Teste JOHN BROWN, C. G. C.
DUMFRIES District Court, October 17th 1793
        ROBERT TOWNSHEND HOOE, WILLIAM BROWN &   ]
        CHARLES SIMMS, Administrators &c. of JOHN MILLS,   ]
        deceased, Plaintiffs   ]   In Case
                against   ]
        CHARLES CHILTON & JOSEPH BLACKWELL, Defendants]
    This suit is dismissed being agreed by the parties

        Arnold v Arnold
        ISAAC ARNOLD, Plaintiff   ]
                against   ]   In Case
        BENJAMIN ARNOLD, Administrator of HUMPHREY ARNOLD]
        deceased. Defendant   ]

ISAAC ARNOLD, Plaintiff]
    against] In Debt
BENJAMIN ARNOLD, Administrator of HUMPHREY ARNOLD]
deceased, Defendant]

These suits are dismissed being agreed by the parties

p.   Tayloe v Hunter
311   The Commonwealth of Virginia to the Sheriff of FAIRFAX County, Greeting.
We command you that you take WILLIAM HUNTER JUNR. if he be found
within your Bailiwick and him safely keep so that you have him before the Judges of
the District Court to be held at the Town of DUMFRIES at the next Court to answer
JOHN TAYLOE, an Infant under the age of twenty one years by MANN PAGE,
FRANCIS LIGHTFOOT LEE, RALPH WORMLEY and WARNER LEWIS his
Guardians, of a Plea of Trespass on the Case, damage four hundred pounds, and have
then there this Writ. Witness GEORGE BROOKE, Clerk of the Court at DUM-
FRIES the 15th day of September in the 15th year of the Commonwealth A.D. 1790
                                  G. BROOKE, C. D. C.

For a breach of Contract. No Bail required
Executed   p BALDWIN DADE
October 17th 1793

JOHN TAYLOE, an Infant under the age of twenty one years]
by MANN PAGE, FRANCIS LIGHTFOOT LEE, RALPH]
WORMLEY and WARNER LEWIS his Guardians, Plaintiffs]
    against] In Case
WILLIAM HUNTER, JUNR. Defendant]

This suit abates by the death of the Defendant

Cawood v Reeder
The Commonwealth of Virginia to the Sheriff of Prince William County,
Greeting. We command you that you take THOMAS REEDER if he be found within
your Bailiwick and him safely keep so that you have his body before the Judges of the
District Court to be held at the Town of DUMFRIES at the next Court to answer
BENJAMIN CAWOOD of a Plea of Debt for one hundred ninety two pounds, nine
shillings and four pence half penny current money of MARYLAND of the value of one
hundred fifty three pounds, nineteen shillings and six pence current money and eight
hundrd ninety two pounds of tobacco, damage ten pounds, and have then there this
Writ; Witness GEORGE BROOKE, Clerk of the Court at DUMFRIES the 28th day
of September in the 15th year of the Commonwealth A. D. 1790
                                  G. BROOKE, C. D. C.

p.   Cawood v Reeder
312   For Debt due by Judgment of the General Court of the Western Shore of
the State of MARYLAND, Bail is required.
Executed   JAMES TRIPLETT, D. S.

FAIRFAX to wit

BENJAMIN CAWOOD complains of THOMAS REEDER in custody &c. of a Plea that he render unto him the sum of one hundred ninety two pounds, nine shillings and four pence half penny current money of MARYLAND of the value of one hundred fifty three pounds, nineteen shillings and six pence current money of Virginia as also the sum of eight hundred ninety two pounds of tobacco which to him he owes and from him he detains for that whereas the Plaintiff at a General Court held at the City of ANNAPOLIS for the Western Shore in MARYLAND on the 12th day of May 1790, obtained a Judgment against the Defendant for the sum of one hundred ninety two pounds, nine shillings and four pence half penny current money of MARLAND of the value aforesaid of Virginia currency as also the sum of eight hundred ninety two pounds of tobacco which to the Plaintiff in the Court were adjudged for his Debt as well for his costs and charges by him the Plaintiff about his suit in that behalf expended, whereof the Defendant is convict as by the Record of the same Court remaining more fully is manifest and appears which Judgment yet remains in full force and effect not satisfied or reversed and the Plaintiff hath not yet sued out his Execution on the Judgment in form aforesaid recovered whereby action has accrued to the Plaintiff to demand and have of the Defendant the sum of money as also the quantity of tobacco, yet the Defendant altho often required the sum of money and tobacco to the Plaintiff hath not yet paid but the same to him to pay hath hitherto altogether refused and still doth reuse to the damage of the Plaintiff [blank] pounds, therefore he brings suit &c.
                                            SIMMS for the Plaintiff

Pledges &c. J. Doe & R. Roe
November 1790   Common Order against Defendant and Sheriff
February & April 1791. Continuance for Declaration
May 1791   Declaration filed, Common Order confirmed and Inquiry
October 17th 1793
Abates, Defendant dead

p.   Forrest & Stoddart v Ramsay
313   The Commonwealth of Virginia to the Sheriff of FAIRFAX County, Greeting.
We command you that you take DENNIS RAMSAY if he be found within your Bailiwick and him safely keep so that you have his body before the Judges of the District Court to be held at the Town of DUMFRIES at the next Court to answer URIAH FORREST and BENJAMIN STODDART of a Plea of Debt for five hundred ninety three pounds, six shillngs and six pence, damage ten pounds, And have then there this Writ. Witness GEORGE BROOKE, Clerk of the Court at DUMFRIES the 28th day of April in the 15th year of the Commonwealth A. D. 1790
                              G. BROOKE,   C. D. C.
For Debt due by Bond. Bail is required
Executed   CHARLES TURNER, Sheriff
FAIRFAX to wit

URIAH FORREST and BENJAMIN STODDART complain of DENNIS RAMSAY in custody &c. of a Plea that he render unto them the just and full sum of five hundred ninety three pounds, six shillings and six pence which to them he owes and from them unjustly detains for that whereas the Defendant on the 28th day of January 1789 at the Parish of Fairfax and County aforesaid by his certain Writing Obligatory sealed with his seal and to the Court now nere shewn, whose date is the same day and year, acknowledged himself to be held and firmly bound unto the Plaintiffs in the sum of five hundred ninety three pounds, six shillings and six pence to be paid to the Plaintiffs when he should be thereunto afterwards required, yet the Defendant altho thereto often required the sum of money or any part thereof to the Plaintiffs or to either of them hath not paid but the same to pay hath hitherto altogether refused and still doth refuse to the damage of the Plaintiffs ten pounds, therefore they bring suit, &c.

SIMMS for the Plaintiffs

Pledges &c. J. Doe & R. Roe
May 1791   Declaration and Bail filed, oyer and Special Imparlance
June 1791   Rule to plead
July 1791   Ruled to Security for costs, payment joined

p.   Forrest & Stoddart v Ramsay
314   Memorandum; That upon the ninth day of May in the year of our Lord one
          thousand seven hundred and ninety one, JOHN FITZGERALD of the County of FAIRFAX personally appeared before me, GEORGE GILPIN, Gentleman, one of the persons appointed by the Honourable General Court for taking Special Bail within the County of FAIRFAX, and undertook for the Defendant, DENNIS RAMSAY, at the suit of URIAH FORREST and BENJAMIN STODDART in a Plea of Debt now depending in the Honourable the District Court at DUMFRIES that in case DENNIS RAMSAY shall be cast in the suit he, DENNIS RAMSAY, will pay and satisfy the condemnation of the Court or render his body to Prison in Execution for the same or that he, JOHN FITZGERALD, will do it for him

GEORGE GILPIN

          KNOW ALL MEN by these presents that I DENNIS RAMSAY of the Town of ALEXANDRIA am held and firmly bound unto URIAH FORREST and BENJAMIN STODDART of GEORGE TOWN in the State of MARYLAND in the just and full sum of five hundred ninety three pounds, six shillings and six pence to which payment well and truly to be made unto URIAH FORREST and BENJAMIN STODDART their heirs Executors, Administrators or assigns I bind myself my heirs Executors and Administrators firmly by these presents, Sealed with my seal and dated this 28th day of January 1789

          THE CONDITION of the above obligation is such that if the above bound DENNIS RAMSAY shall well and truly pay unto URIAH FORREST and BENJAMIN STODDART their Executors Administrators or assigns the sum of two hundred ninety six pounds, thirteen shillings and three pence on or before the first day of January in the year one thousand sven hundred and ninety one with Interest thereon from the date herof, then the above Obligation to be void otherwise to remain in full force power and virtue

Sealed and delivered in presence of
    CHARLES SIMMS   DENNIS RAMSAY
    HENRY LEE
October 17th 1793

p.   Forrest & Stoddart v Ramsay
315   URIAH FORREST & BENJAMIN STODDART, Plaintiffs   ]
                        against   ] In Debt
        DENNIS RAMSAY, Defendant   ]
   This day came the parties by their Attornies and the Defendant relinquishing his
former Plea acknowledged the Plaintiffs's action against him; therefore it is considered by the Court that the Plaintiffs recover against the Defendant five hundred
ninety three pounds, six shillings and six pence, the Debt in the Declaration mentioned and their costs by them about their suit in this behalf expended and the Defendant in mercy, &c. But this Judgment may be discharged by the payment of two
hundred ninety six pounds, thirteen shillings and three pence with Interest thereon to
be computed after the rate of five percentum per annum from the 28th day of
January 1789 till paid and the costs
        Costs   30 lbs tobacco @ 1 1/2   ]
                160 lbs tobacco @ 1 1/4   ] p pound & $ 7.34.
        Execution issued

        Haynes & Crawford v Fitzgerald
        The Commonwealth of Virginia to the Sheriff of FAIRFAX County, Greeting.
We command you that you take JOHN FITZGERALD if he be found within your
Bailiwick and him safely keep so that you have his body before the Judges of the
District Court to be held at the Town of DUMFRIES at the next Court to answer
GEORGE HAYNES and JAMES CRAWFORD under the name of HAYNES &
CRAWFORD of a Plea of Trspass on the Case, damage four hundred pounds, And
that then and there have this Writ. Witness GEORGE BROOKE, Clerk of the Court
at DUMFRIES the 21st day of October in the 15th year of the Commonwealth A. D.
1790
                                G. BROOKE, C. D. C.
        For money due by Account.
                        CHARLES LEE, for Plaintiffs
        Executed   p BALDWIN DADE

FAIRFAX County, to wit
        GEORGE HAYNES and JAMES CRAWFORD under the Firm of HAYNES &
CRAWFORD, Merchants, complain of JOHN FITZGERALD in custody & so forth for
this to wit that whereas the Defendant on the sixth day of December in the year 1785
at the Parish of Fairfax and County aforesaid was

p.   Haynes & Crawford v Fitzgerald
316   indebted in the sum of six hundred pounds lawful money of PENSYLVANIA
        of the value of four hundred eighty pounds Virginia currency for so much
money lent and advanced by the Plaintiffs to the Defendant at his special instance
and request and being so indebted in consideration thereof the Defendant then and
there in consideration thereof assumed upon himself and promised faithfully to pay to
the Plaintiffs the sum of four hundred eighty pounds lawful money of Virginia when he

should be thereto required and whereas afterwards to with on the [blank] day of [blank] in the year 1786 at the Parish and County aforesaid, the Defendant was indebted to the Plaintiffs in another sum of four hundred eighty pounds lawfull money of Virginia for so much money before that time had and received by the Defendant for the use of the Plaintiffs and being so indebted in consideration thereof the Defendant then and there promised to the Plaintiffs and assumed upon himself to faithfully pay to them, the Plaintiffs, the sum of four hundred and eighty pounds when he should be thereunto required; Nevertheless the Defendant though often thereafter required not regarding his promises made as aforesaid but contriving to defraud the Plaintiffs in these particulars hath not paid to them the sums of money or any part thereof but hitherto hath refused and still doth refuse to pay the same to them to the Plaintiffs's damage four hundred pounds and therefore they sue &c.

CHARLES LEE for Plaintiffs

Pledges of prosecution, John Doe & R. Roe

May 1791   Common Order

June 1791   WILLIAM LOWRY Security for costs & continued for Declaration

July 1791   Declaration filed, Common Order confirmed & Inquiry

DR. JOHN FITZGERALD, Esqr., in an Account with HAYNES & CRAWFORD

1784	July 27	To MOORE & CRAWFORD Bill on SAMUEL W. BROWN	100
	November 9	do	100
1785	February 15	do	100
	May 10	do	100
	August 23	do	100
	December 6	do	100
			600.....0.....0.

p. 317   Haynes & Crawford v Fitzgerald

	January 18	By Burwell, Basset on Hyndeman & Co. L. 50 @ 74 p c 87		
	"	By his Order on do.	17.5	104.....5.....0
	January 28	By Donaldson & Coxes Assumption		34.....4.....4
	December 6	By nett proceeds of hhds. tobacco p Sloop Channing Mary		141...17.....9
1788	February 13	By Balance		319...12...11
				600.....0.....0

I believe the last Bill for one hundred pounds paid by Mr. Brown, I am sure he paid all the rest and I credited him for the five hundred pounds in account, Mr. FITZGERALD can clear up this matter by delivering up MOORE & CRAWFORD's last draft which should be done before the exact balance is ascertained upwards of four years Interest now due

PHILADELPHIA, 2d May 1790

Sir. I beg leave through the introduction of Mr. GILCHRIST to trouble you with the enclosed account upon which you will please to institute a suit against Mr. FITZGERALD immediately in the District Court

I have been endeavouring to get this money from Mr. F. for the two last years through the interception of four or five different Merchants and remonstrated to him against such unjustifiable conduct as holding money received confidentially in trust for so many years, but he will not answer letters or give the smallest satisfaction. I have wrote Messrs. LOWRY & CO. requesting to give you a proper fee upon the occasion and security if necessary for costs

You will see by the Draft of one hundred pounds   Respectfully
which Mr. F. will return whether the Bills were   Your very Obedient Servant
for Virginia or PENSYLVANIA currency, if the   HUGH MOORE
former it will make our demand so much more,
the Credits I know are PENSYLVANIA money. If Mr. F. will give security for payment in a short time I will be satisfied such a settlement will be more to his honour and agreeable to you

LEE, Esquire, ALEXANDRIA

Messrs. LOWRY & CO.   PHILADELPHIA 2d May 1790
     Gentlemen. As I find it will be disagreeable with you to undertake a suit against Mr. FITZGERALD, I have got a friend here to introduce me to Mr.

p.   Haynes & Crawford v Fitzgerld
318   LEE [a Gentleman of the Law] I will thank you to give Mr. LEE a proper fee
     upon the occasion and security if necessary for the costs of suit. You may take your reimbursment as most agreeable either on Mr. ABERNATHY or your most obedient servant,
Messrs. LOWRY & CO.   HUGH MOORE
       Merchants, ALEXANDRIA

PHILADELPHIA 24th July 1790

     Sir. I am favoured with your letter of the 20th intstant and am obliged for your application to Colo. FITZGERALD. I observe he has promised to pay the balance due to HAYNES & CRAWFORD in two months but he objectes to their statement and has promised to furnish an Account from his Books which it will be necessary for us to have as soon as possible that errors [if any] may be rectified in time for next Term. The last Bill drawn by Mr. CRAWFORD and me on Mr. BROWN was I believe not paid as I mentioned in my last letter but that he can clear up by delivering you up our draft. Interest is a just charge he can have no objection to and I dare say that the Credits given upon the whole as this is the first we have heard of this objection. I immagine the Accounts will be found right.
CHARLES LEE Esqr.   I am respectfully, Sir
                                   Your obedient Servant
                                   HUGH MOORE

PHILADELPHIA 4th October 1790

CHARLES LEE, Esqr. Sir. I took the liberty of addressing you a letter under the 18th ulta. it was delivered to a Gentleman who promised to put it in the Post Office at BALTIMORE but as I have not had an answer I shall conclude it has miscarried and repeat the contents.
     Mr. FITZGERALD [by your Letter of 20th Jul] it appears you promised to pay in two months [say 20th ulta] and if he did not you were to sue him. As he has not furnished any Account contradicting the one sent you, it must be right except as to my last draft for one hundred pounds which was sent him for collection but I believe

was not paid, this can be

p.   Haynes & Crawford v Fitzgerald
319   cleared up by his returning the Bill itself. You will take care of the Interest it
        is fair to charge.   I am respectfully
Specie by a safe conveyance bank   Sir, your Obedient Servant
Notes or a Draft of PHILADELPHIA   HUGH MOORE
will be a good remittance if you secure
CHARLES LEE, Esqr. ALEXANDRIA

October 17th 1793.
        GEORGE HAYNES & JAMES CRAWFORD, under the name   ]
        HAYNES & CRAWFORD, Plaintiffs   ]
                against   ] In Case
        JOHN FITZGERALD, Defendant   ]
     This day came the Plaintiffs by their Attorney and thereupon a Jury to wit
        JOHN MANDEVILLE   JOHN COOK   GEORGE BRENT
        DAVID BOYLE   WILLIAM SCOTT   ALEXANDER ANDERSON
        HUGH STUART   LUND WASHINGTON   THOMAS LEE
        WILLIAM REED   SAMUEL TEBBS and WILLOUGHBY TEBBS
being sworn well and truly to inquire of damages in this suit, upon their Oath do say
that the Plaintiffs have sustained damaged by means of the Defendant's breach of
the promise and assumption in the Declaration mentioned to two hundred ninety five
pounds, nine shillings besides their costs; therefore it is considered by the Court that
the Plaintiffs recover against the Defendants their damages in form assessed and
their costs by them about their suit in this behalf expended and the Defendant in
mercy &.
        Costs   30 lbs. tobacco @ 1 1/2   ]
                130 lbs tobacco @ 1 1/4   ] p pound & $10.50
        Execution issued

p.   Bennett v Herbert
320   The Commonwealth of Virginia to the Sheriff of FAIRFAX County, Greeting
        We command you that you take THOMAS HERBERT if he be found within
your Bailiwick and him safely keep so that you have his body before the Judges of the
District Court to be held at the Town of DUMFRIES at the next Court to answer
HENRY ASTLEY BENNETT, Esqr. of a Plea of Trespass on the Case, damage two
thousand pounds, and have then there this Writ. Witness GEORGE BROOKE, Clerk
of the Court at DUMFRIES the 17th day of August in the 15th year of the Commonwealth A. D. 1790
                                G. BROOKE, C. D. C.
        For diverting and turning the water from the Plaintiff's Grist Mill whereby it
was rendered useless
        Executed p BALDWIN DADE
FAIRFAX County, to wit
        HENRY ASTLEY BENNETT Esqr. complains of THOMAS HERBERT in
custody, &c. for that whereas the Plaintiff on the [blank] day of [blank] in the year
17[blank] and before was seized of and in a certain tract of land with its appurte-

nances lying and being in the Parish of [blank] and County aforesaid together with all waters and water courses whatsoever thro which tract of land a certain Run by the name of [blank] on the day and year aforesaid did turn and long before to wit from time whereof the memory of man runneth not to the contrary was continually accustomed to run and whereas also the Plaintiff being so seized as aforesaid of the tract of land and appurtenances in the Parish and County aforesaid did afterwards to wit on the [blank] day of [blank] in the year 17[blank] upon the Run build erect and perfect a Grist Mill for the purpose of grinding Wheat & Corn by reason whereof the Plaintiff then was seized and as yet is seized of the Grist Mill in his demsne of fee and the Grist Mill was worked by the waters of the Run which from the time of erecting building and perfecting the Grist Mill untill the [blank] day of [blank] in the year 17[blank] did run there by reason whereof the Plaintiff after the building of the Grist Mill until the [blank] day of [blank] last mentioned

p. <u>Bennett v Herbert</u>
321 in the year last mentioned had gotten divers gains and profits of the Neighbours and other persons bringing their Wheat and Corn there to be ground and manufactured at the Grist Mill, yet the Defendant well knowing the premises maliciously diverting and intending the Plaintiff to molest and him altogether to hinder and deprive of the profits of the Grist Mill at the Parish aforesaid in the County aforesaid on the [blank] day of [blank] in the year abovesaid the stream of water which to the Grist Mill did run and ought to run from its ancient and used course did divert and withdraw whereby the Plaintiff the whole profit of his Grist Mill for a great time, that is to say from the aforesaid [blank] day of [blank] in the year last mentioned untill this present day wholly lost to the damage of the Plaintiff [blank] pounds, therefore he brings suit &c.

SIMMS for the Plaintiff

Pledges &c. J. Doe & R. Roe

November 1790	Common Order
December 1790	Common Order set aside and Special Imparlance
January 1791	Rule to declare
February 1791	Continued for Declaration
April 1781	ditto
May 1791	Declaration filed
June 1791	Rule to plead
July 1791	Continued for Plea
August 1791	Judgment by Nihil Dicit and Inquiry
October 1791	Referred

ALEXANDRIA, October 8th 1791

Sir. You are requested to obtain an Order of the DUMFRIES District Court to refer the suit therein depending brought in the name of HENRY ASTLEY BENNETT against THOMAS HERBERT for turning the water &c. from HENRY ASTLEY BENNETT's Mill on HOLMES RUN to RICHARD CONWAY and DAVID STUART and to discontinue the Appeal of HENRY ASTLEY BENNETT from the Judgment of the County Court of FAIRFAX granting leave to THOMAS HERBERT to erect a Mill on HOLMES RUN

CHARLES SIMMS, Esqr.　　　　　　　THOMAS　HERBERT
　　& LUDWELL LEE, Esqr.　　　　　R. T. HOOE
　　　　　　　　　　　　　　　　　CHARLES　LITTLE

DUMFRIES October District Court 1791
　　HENRY ASTLEY BENNETT, Plaintiff　　　　　　]
　　　　　　against　　　　　　　　　　　　　　] In Case
　　THOMAS　HERBERT, Defendant　　　　　　　]
　　The parties by their Attornies mutually submit all matters in difference between them relative to this suit to the determination of RICHARD CONWAY and DAVID STUART and their award is to be made the Judgment of the Court

October 17th 1793
　　　　This day came the parties by their Attornies and the Referees returned their award which was ordered to be recorded and is in these words, to wit;
　　"In Obedience to the annexed Order of the District Court of DUMFRIES we the Subscribers did on the twenty eighth day of June 1793 at the request of the parties repair to the premises in dispute and there heard testimony on both sides and on examining the several papers exhibited to us relative thereto and duly considering the proofs and allegations of both the parties do make the following award; That the suit be dismissed and the Plaintiff pay all costs. Given under our hands and seals the 29th day of June 1793. RICHD. CONWAY, [seal] DAVID STUART [seal]"
　　Therefore it is considered by the Court that the Plaintiff take nothing by his Bill but for his false clamours be in mercy &c., and that the Defendant go thereof without day and recover against the Plaintiff his costs by him about his defence in this behalf expended
　　　　Defendant's costs　55 lbs tobacco @ 1 1/4 & $4.16.

p.　　Wallace & Muir v Brown
323　　The Commonwealth of Virginia to the Sheriff of Prince William County,
　　　　Greeting. We command you that you take ALEXANDER BROWN if he be found within your Bailiwick and him safely keep so that you have his body before the Judges of the District Court to be held at the Town of DUMFRIES at the next Court to answer WALLACE & MUIR of a Plea of Debt for one thousand four hundred nine pounds, seven shillings and six pence, damage five pounds, And have then there this Writ. Witness GEORGE BROOKE, Clerk of the Court at DUMFRIES the first day of March in the 14th year of the Commonwealth A. D. 1790
　　　　　　　　　　　　　　　　G.　BROOKE　　　C. D. D. C.
　　On Bond, Bail required　　J. MINOR for Plaintiff
　　June 1790　　　　　　Common Order against Defendant & Sheriff
　　August 1790　　　　　Continued for Declaration
　　February 1791　　　　　do
　　April 1791　　　　　　do
　　May 1791　　　　　Common Order confirmed and Inquiry
Prince William County, to wit
　　WALLACE & MUIR complain of ALEXANDER BROWN in custody &c. of a

Plea that they render unto them one thousand four hundred nine pounds, seven shillings and six pence Virginia currency which he owes to them and unjustly detains for this to wit that whereas ALEXANDER BROWN on the sixth day of May 1788 at Prince William County by his certain Writing Obligatory sealed with his seal and to the Court now here shewn, the date whereof is on the same day and year aforesaid, did acknowledge himself to be held and firmly bound to the Plaintiffs in the sum of one thousand four hundred nine pounds, seven shilllings and six pence Virginia currency to be paid to the Plaintiffs on demand, yet the Defendant altho often required has not yet paid the one thousand four hundred nine pounds, seven shillings and six pence to the Plaintiffs but hitherto to pay the same hath refused and still doth refuse to the damage of the Plaintiffs of five pounds and therefore they bring suit, &c.

J. MINOR for Plaintiff

KNOW ALL MEN by these presents that I ALEXANDER BROWN of Prince William County and State of Virginia am held and firmly bound unto

p.   Wallace & Muir v Brown
324   Messrs WALLACE & MUIR in the just and full sum of one thousand four hundred nine pence, seven shillings and six pence Virginia currence to be paid to Messrs. WALLACE & MUIR their certain Attorney their heirs Executors Administrators or assigns to which payment well and truly to be made I bind myself my heirs Executors and Administrators firmly by these presents, Sealed with my seal and dated this sixth day of May Anno Dom one thousand seven hundred eighty eight

THE CONDITION of the above Obligation is such that if the above bound ALEXANDER BROWN his heirs Executors Administrators or assigns do and shall well and truly pay or cause to be paid unto Messrs. WALLACE & MUIR their certain Attorney their heirs Executors Administrators or assigns the just sum of seven hundred four pounds, thirteen shillings and nine pence currency in specie on or before the thirteenth day of December next then the above Obligation to be void or else to remain in full force and virtue

Sealed and delivered n presence of

JOHN DALRYMPLE   ALEXR. BROWN   [seal]

This is to certify that I paid to WALLACE & MUIR of ANOPOLIS on the 9th day of June 1792 for Mr. ALEXANDER BROWN one hundred pounds current money

JAMES MUSCHETT

The within mentioned sum of eighty hundred one dollars was received on the first day of June 1793 and placed to the Credit of Mr. A. BROWN to WALLACE & MUIR

RICHARD M. SCOTT
The 16th October 1793

October 17th 1793

<table>
<tr><td>WALLACE & MUIR, Plaintiffs
against
ALEXANDER BROWN, Defendant</td><td>]
]
]</td><td>In Debt</td></tr>
</table>

This day came the Plaintiffs by their Attorney and by their consent the Writ of Inquiry awarded in this suit is set aside and the Defendant in his proper person came and acknowledged the Plaintiffs's action against him; therefore it is considered by the

Court that the Plaintiffs recover against the Defendant one thousand four hundred nine pounds, seven shillings and six pence Virginia currency, the Debt in the Declaration mentioned, and their costs by them

p.   Wallace & Muir v Brown
325   about their suit in this behalf expended, and the Defendant in mercy, &c., But this Judgment may be discharged by the payment of seven hundred four pounds, thirteen shillings and nine pence currency in specie with Interest thereon to be computed after the rate of five per centum per annum from the ninth day of June 1793

Costs 75 lbs tobacco @ 1 1/2   ]
      85 lbs tobacco @ 1 1/4   ] p pounds & $8.34

Davidson v Boggess
The Commonwealth of Virginia to the Sheriff of FAIRFAX County, Greeting; We command you that you take ROBERT BOGGESS if he be found within your Bailiwick and him safely keep so that you have his body before the Judges of the District Cout to be held at the Town of DUMFRIES at the next Court to answer SAMUEL DAVIDSON of a Plea of Trespass upon the Case, damage one hundred pounds, and have then there this Writ. Witness GEORGE BROOKE, Clerk of the Court at DUMFRIES this 28th day of April in the 15th year of the Commonwealth A. D. 1790

G. BROOKE, C. D. C.

For money due by Account.
Executed per GEORGE MINOR, S S

FAIRFAX County to wit
SAMUEL DAVIDSON complains of ROBERT BOGGESS in cutody, &c., for this to wit that whereas the Defendant on the 31st day of December 1790 at the Parish of [blank] and County aforesaid was indebted to the Plaintiff the sum of seventy six pounds, eleven shillings and eleven pence current money of MARYLAND of the value of sixty one pounds, five shillings and six pence half penny current money of Virginia for divers goods wares and merchandize to the Defendant by the Plaintiff at the special instance and request of the Defendant before that time there sold and delivered; and so being therein indebted he, the Defendant, in consideration thereof afterwards, to wit, the same day and year at the

p.   Davidson v Boggess
326   County aforesaid assumed upon himself to the Plaintiff then and there faithfully promised that the Defendant the seventy six pounds, eleven shillings and eleven pence current money of the value aforesaid in Virginia currency to the Plaintiff when he should be thereto afterwards required would well and truly pay and satisfy and whereas also the Defendant afterwards to wit the day and year abovesaid at the Parish and County aforesaid in consideration that the Plaintiff at the like special instance and request of the Defendant before that time had then sold and delivered to the Defendant divers other goods wares and merchandize assumed upon himself and

and to the Plaintiff then and there faithfully promised tht he, the Defendant, so much money as the goods wares and merchandize las mentioned were reasonably worth at the time of the sales and delivery thereof to the Plaintiff when he should be thereto afterwards required would well and truly pay and content and the Plaintiff avers that the goods wares and merchandize mentioned were reasonably worth at the time of the sale and delivery thereof other seven six pounds, eleven shillings and eleven pence current money of MARYLAND of the value of sixty one pounds, five shillings and six pence half penny Virginia currency whereof the Defendant the day year and place last mentioned had notice; Nevertheless the Defendant his several promises and assumptions in form aforesaid made not regarding but contriving and fraudulently intending the Plaintiff in this behalf craftily and subtlely to deceive and defraud hath not yet paid the several sums of money or any penny thereof to the Plaintiff altho thereto often required but he hitherto hath altogether refused and still doth refuse to the damage of the Plaintiff one hundred pounds and therefore he brings suit, &c.

SIMMS for the Plaintiff

Pledges &c. J. Doe & R. Roe
May 1791   Declaration filed and Common Order
June 1791   Common Order confirmed and Inquiry

p.   Davidson v Boggess
327   Mr. ROBERT BOGGESS to SAMUEL DAVIDSON   DR.
[There follows on this page a schedule of the goods wares and merchandize purchased by ROBERT BOGGESS of SAMUEL DAVIDSON, 24 August 1789, 27 October 1789; 18 November 1789 and 22 December 1789, being the kinds of goods and wares one would expect to find in a purchase made by one merchant of another.]

p.   Davidson v Boggess
328   1790. December 31. To Interest Account for amount due on
          L. 16.....5.....9, from 1st of March last to this date   0...16.....3
          On L. 57...15...7, from 1st July last to this date   1...14.....4
                                                                        2...10.....7
              Total MARYLAND Currency   L. 76...11...11
GEORGE TOWN 31st December 1790
              Errors Excepted   SAM: DAVIDSON
State of MARYLAND, MONTGOMERY County, 11 January 1791
      I hereby certify that the foregoing Account is a true copy from the Books of Accounts of SAMUEL DAVIDSON which Books are proved according to Law at the same time SAMUEL DAVIDSON made Oath that the same is just and true and that he hath not directly or indirectly received any part or parcel thereof nor any thing in Security or satisfaction for the same to the best of his knowledge
              Certified by and sworn before me
              SAML: W. MAGRUDER
      State of MARYLAND, MONTGOMERY County to wit. I do hereby certify SAMUEL W. MAGRUDER, Gentleman, who appears to have signed the within certificate was at the time of signing thereof and still is one of the Justices of the Peace for the County aforesaid duly commissioned and sworn &c. to whose acts as such due faith and credit is and ought to be given as well in Courts of Justice as thereout
[SEAL]   In Testimony whereof I have hereunto set my hand and seal of my

Office this eleventh day of January Anno Domini 1791
                    BROOKE BEALL, Clk.
October 17th 1793
        SAMUEL DAVIDSON, Plaintiff   ]
              against   ] In Case
        ROBERT BOGGESS, Defendant   ]
This day came the Plaintiff by his Attorney and thereupon a Jury, to wit
        LANGHORNE DADE   WILLIAM MARSHALL   CHARLES MARSHALL
        JOHN MINOR   OBEDIAH PETTIT   GEORGE WILLIAMS
        THOMAS JAMES   WILLOUGHBY TEBBS   JAMES TRIPLETT
        LUND WASHINGTON   WILLIAM TYLER   and RICHARD FOOTE
being sworn well and truly to inquire of damages in this suit upon their Oath do say
the the Plaintiff hath sustained damages by means of the Defendant's breach of the
promise and assumption in the Declaration

p.   Davidson v Boggess
329`   mentioned to sixty six pounds, twelve shillings and three pence besides his
        costs; therefore it is considered by the Court that the Plaintiff recover against
the Defendant his damages in form assessed and his costs by him about his suit in
this behalf expended, and the Defendant in mercy, &c.
        Costs   30 lbs tobacco @ 1 1/2   ]
                130 lbs tobacco @ 1 1/4   ] p pound & $9.90
        Execution issued

        Graham v Atwell's Admors.
        The Commonwealth of Virginia to the Sheriff of Prince William County
Greeting; We command you that you take CHARLES ATWELL and ANNA
ATWELL, Administrators of THOMAS ATWELL, deceased, if they be found within
your Bailiwick and them safely keep so that you have their bodies before the Judges
of the District Court to be held at the Town of DUMFRIES at the next Court to
answer RICHARD GRAHAM of a Plea of Debt for thirteen thousand seven hundred
ninety six pounds of crop tobacco, damage three hundred pounds, and have then there
this Writ. Witness GEORGE BROOKE, Clerk of the Court at DUMFRIES the third
day of May in the 15th year of the Commonwealth A. D. 1791
                    G. BROOKE, C. D. C.
        Executed on CHARLES ATWELL and a Copy left at MRS. ATWELL's
                    HENRY BROWN, D. S.

        The Commonwealth of Virginia to the Sheriff of Prince William County
Greeting; We command you as we have at another time commanded you that you
take ANN ATWELL, Administratrix of THOMAS ATWELL deceased, if she be found
within your Bailiwick and her safely keep so that you have her body before the Judges
of the District Court to be held at the Town of DUMFRIES at the next Court to
answer RICHARD GRAHAM of a Plea of Debt for ninety three pounds and six pence
current money, damage twenty pounds, and have then there this Writ. Witness
GEORGE BROOKE, Clerk of the Court at DUMFRIES the 13th day of June in the

15th year of the Commonwealth A. D. 1791

G. BROOKE, C. D. C.

Executed. HENRY BROWN, D. Sh.

p.   Graham v Atwell's Admors.
330   Prince William County, to wit

RICHARD GRAHAM complains of CHARLES ATWELL and ANN ATWELL Administrators of THOMAS ATWELL, deceased, in custody, of a Plea that they render to him the sum of thirteen thousand seven hundred ninety six pounds of crop tobacco which to him they owe and from him unjustly detain for that whereas THOMAS ATWELL in his life time, to wit, on the fourth day of March in the yar of our Lord 1784 at the Parish of [blank] in the County aforesaid by his certain Writing Obligatory sealed with his seal and to the Court now here shewn, the date whereof is the same day and year aforesaid, acknowledged himself to be held and firmly bound unto RICHARD GRAHAM in the just and full sum of thirteen thousand seven hundred ninety six pounds of crop tobacco to be paid to RICHARD GRAHAM whenever he should be thereunto afterwards required, Nevertheless THOMAS ATWELL altho often thereto required in his life tme and the Defendants, CHARLES ATWELL and ANN ATWELL, his Administrators, altho thereto often required since the death of THOMAS have not nor hath either of them paid the sum of tobacco or any part thereof to RICHARD but the same to pay have hitherto refused and still doth refuse to the damage of RICHARD three hundred pounds, therefore he brings suit &c.

BRENT for the Plaintiff

Pledges &c. J. Doe & R. Roe

May 1791	Common Order against CHARLES ATWELL and alias capias against other
June 1791	Continuance for Declaration
July 1791	ditto
August 1791	Common Order confirmed and Inquiry
October 1791	Common Order against Defendant
November 1791	Common Order confirmed
May 1792	Common Order set aside and payment joined

KNOW ALL MEN by these presents that I THOMAS ATWELL of Prince William County am held and firmly bound unto RICHARD GRAHAM of DUMFRIES in the just and full sum of thirteen thousand seven hundred and ninety six pounds of crop tobacco to be paid unto RICHARD GRAHAM his

p.   Graham v Atwell's Admors.
331   certain Attorney his heirs Executors Administrators or assigns to which payment well and truly to be made I bind myself my heirs Executors and Administrators firmly by these presents; sealed with my seal and dated this fourth day of March Anno Dom one thousand seven hundred and eighty four

THE CONDITION of the above Obligation is such that if the above bound THOMAS ATWELL shall well and truly pay or cause to be paid unto RICHARD GRAHAM his certain Attorney his Executors Administrators or assigns the sum of six thousand eight hundred forty eight pounds of crop tobacco and cask on DUM-

FRIES of QUANTICO WAREHOUSEs on demand then the above Obligation to be void or else to remain in full force and virtue
Sealed and delivered in presence of
RICHARD SCOTT   THOS: ATWELL   [seal]

October 18th 1793

RICHARD GRAHAM, Plaintiff   ]
      against   ] In Debt
CHARLES ATWELL & ANNA ATWELL, Administrators]
of THOMAS ATWELL, deceased, Defendants   ]

This day came the Plaintiff by his Attorney and thereupon a Jury, to wit

EDWARD MINTER	JAMES SMITH	WILLIAM BAILEY
MOSES BAILEY	NATHANIEL TRIPLETT	THOMAS THORNTON
ANTHONY BUCKNER	JOHN MAUZY	GUSTAVUS BOSWELL
JAMES BOOTH	REUBIN WARE and	RODHAM KENNER

being sworn well and truly to inquire of damages in this suit upon their Oath do say that the Plaintiff hath sustained damages by means of the detention of that debt to one penny besides his costs; thereupon it is considered by the Court tht the Plaintiff recover against the Defendants thirteen thousand seven hundred and ninety six pounds of crop tobacco, the Debt in the Declaration mentioned, together with his damages in form assessed and his costs by him about his suit in this behalf expended to be levied of the goods and chattles of the deceased at the time of his death in the hands of the Defendants to be administered if so much thereof in their hands they have but if not then the costs to be levied of their own proper goods and chattles and the Defendants in mercy, &c., but this Judgment may be discharged by the payment of six thousand eight hundred forty eight pounds of crop tobacco on DUMFRIES or QUANTICO WAREHOUSEs with Interest thereon to be computed after the rate of five per centum per annum from the fourth day of March 1784 untill paid and the damages and costs

    Costs 60 lbs tobacco @ 1 1/2   ]
             210 lbs tobacco @ 1 1/4] p pound & $7.63.
    Execution issued

p.   Muse v Wailes
332   The Commonwealth of Virginia to the Sheriff of FAIRFAX County, Greeting.
       We command you that you take ANDREW WAILES if he be found within your Bailiwick and him safely keep so that you have his body before the Judges of the District Court to be held at the Town of DUMFRIES at the next Court to answer BATTILE MUSE of a Plea of Debt for six hundred fifty two pounds current money, damage ten pounds, and have then there this Writ. Witness GEORGE BROOKE, Clerk of the Court at DUMFRIES this 28th day of April in the 15th year of the Commonwealth A. D. 1790
                    G. BROOKE   C. D. C.
For Debt due by Bond, Bail is required
Executed, ROBERT LYLE and SAMUEL McLANE Appearance Bail
          CHARLES TURNER, D,. Sheriff

KNOW ALL MEN by these presents that we ANDREW WAILES, ROBERT

LYLE and SAMUEL McLANE of FAIRFAX County and State of Virginia are held and firmly bound unto CHARLES LITTLE, Sheriff of FAIRFAX County in the just and full sum of fifteen hundred pounds current money of Virginia to be paid to CHARLES LITTLE his Executors Administrators or assigns to which payment well and truly to be made we bind ourselves and each of us and each of our heirs Executors and Administrators firmly by these presents; Sealed with our seals and dated this 4th day of May 1790

Whereas BATTAILE MUSE hath sued forth against ANDREW WAILES out of the District Court holden at DUMFRIES a Writ of capias ad respondendum in a Plea of Debt for six hundred fifty two pounds, damage ten pounds, directed to the Sheriff of the County of FAIRFAX which hath been executed upon ANDREW WAILES

Now the Condition of the above Obligation is such that if the above bound ANDREW WAILES do make his personal appearance at the next Court to be held for the District at the Courthouse in DUMFRIES on the first day of the next Court and do then and there abide by fulfill and perform such Orders as by the Court shall be made in the action and do not depart from the Court till the same shall be performed, then the above Obligation to be void or else to remain in full force and virtue in Law

Signed and delivered in the presenceof
CHARLES TURNER

ANDREW WAILES   [seal]
ROBERT LYLE   [seal]
SAMUEL McLANE   [seal]

p.   Muses v Wailes
333   FAIRFAX, to wit

BATTAILE MUSE complains of ANDREW WAILES in custody &c., of a Plea that he render unto him the just and full sum of six hundred fifty two pounds Virginia money which to him he owes and from him unjustly detains for that whereas the Defendant on the 1st day of July 1790 at the Parish of Fairfax and County aforesaid by his certain Writing Obligatory sealed with his seal and to the Court now here shewn whose date is the same day and year, acknowledged himself to be held and firmly bound unto the Plaintiff in the sum of six hundred fifty two pounds Virginia money to be paid to the Plaintiff when the Defendant should be thereunto afterwards required, yet the Defendant altho thereto often required the sum of money or any penny thereof to the Plaintiff hath not paid but the same to him to pay hath hitherto altogether refused and still doth refuse to the damage of the Plaintiff ten pounds, therefore he brings suit, &c.

SIMMS for the Plaintiff

Pledges &c. J. Doe & R. Roe
May 1791   Declaration filed, Common Order against Defendant and
                  Security
June 1791   Common Order confirmed
October 1791   Special Bail, Common Order set aside and payment joined

KNOW ALL MEN by these presents that I ANDREW WAILES of the Town of ALEXANDRIA and State of Virginia am held and firmly bound unto BATTAILE

MUSE of BERKELEY County and State aforesaid in the full and just sum of six hundred fifty two pounds Virginia money on demand to be paid to BATTAILE MUSE his certain Attorney Executors Administrators or assigns to the which payment well and truly to be paid we bind ourselves our heirs Executors and Administrators firmly by these presents; Sealed with our seals and dated the first day of July in the year of our Lord one thousand seven hundred and ninety

THE CONDITION of the above Obligation is such that if the above bound ANDREW EAILES do and shall well and truly paid or cause to be paid unto BATTAILE MUSE his certain Attorney, Executors Administrators or assigns the full and just sum of three hundred twenty six pounds being the

p.   Muse v Wailes
334   ballance due BATTAILE MUSE this day to be paid at or upon demand with
        lawful Interest from this date then the above Obligation to be void or else to
remain in force and virtue in Law
Sealed and delivered in the presence of
        WILLIAM HUNTER, JUNR.   ANDREW WAILES   [seal]
        JOHN M. CARSON

18th October 1793
        This day came the parties by their Attornies and thereupon came a Jury to wit
        EDWARD MINTER   JAMES SMITH   WILLIAM BAILEY
        MOSES BAILEY   NATHANIEL TRIPLETT   THOMAS THORNTON
        ANTHONY BUCKNER   JOHN MAUZY   GUSTAVUS BOSWELL
        JAMES BOOTH   REUBEN WARE   and   RODHAM KENNER
who being elected tried and sworn the truth to speak upon the issue joined upon their Oath do say that the Defendant hath not paid the debt in the Declaration mentioned as by replying the Plaintiff has alledged and they do assess the Plaintiff's damages by reason of the detention of that debt to one penny, besides his costs; therefore it is considered by the Court that the Plaintiff recover against the Defendant six hundred fifty two pounds Virginia currency, the Debt in the Declaration mentioned, and his costs by him about his suit in this behalf expended and the Defendant in mercy &c., But this Judgment may be discharged by the payment of three hundred twenty six pounds with Interest thereon to be computed after the rate of five per centum per annum from the first day of July 1790 untill paid and the damages and costs
        Damages & costs 30 lbs tobacco @ 1 1/2; 150 @ 1 1/4, p pound, & $7.55.
October 22d 1793
        On the motion of ANDREW WAILES an Appeal is granted him from a Judgment obtained against him this Term by BATTAILE MUSE to the Court of Appeals, ANDREW WAILES with DENNIS RAMSAY and LEWIS WESTON his Securities having executed and acknowledged Bond as the Law directs

[Prince William County District Court Order Book, 1793, Dumfries District Court October 1793, will continue in another book, beginning on page 335 with the suit of SAMUEL DAVIDSON against ABRAHAM BARNES THOMPSON MASON.]

KEITH.
Alexander 47,
Mr. 53, 54,
KENNER.
Rodham 109, 111.
KINCHELOE.
Wildman 34, 35, 54,
KING.
Osborn, Dep Sheriff Loudoun Co. 14, 15, 57,
72-74, 85.

LACEY.
Joseph of Loudoun Co. 88-92,
LANGFITT
John 80, 82,
LARROWE.
Isaac, Dep Sheriff Loudoun Co. 21,
LAWSON.
John 47,
William 47,
LEE
Charles, Attorney 15, 25, 45, 46, 52, 53, 55, 65,
72, 78-81, 99-101,
Francis Lightfoot, Gdn of John Tayloe 95,
Henry 97,
Henry, Esqr. of Westmoreland Co. 64, 65,
Ludwell 26, 103,
Thomas 101,
Thomas Senr. 36, 37,
LEWIS.
John of Spotsylvania Co. 22-24,
Joseph 49,
Mordecai & Co. 6-14, 17-19, 56-58, 82-87,
Thomas, Senr. 25, 26, 36, 37,
Warner, Gdn. John Tayloe 95.
LINDSAY.
George W. 22,
Walker 21, 22,
William Junr. 21,
LITHGOW.
Alexander 47,
LITTLE.
Charles 103,
Charles, Sheriff Fairfax Co. 110,
LITTLEJOHN
John of Loudoun Co. 14-16, 74-77,
LOVE.
John of Pr. William Co. 12-14, 32, 33, 59, 60, 64,
65, 77,
Samuel of Pr. William Co. 13, 32-34, 60-62, 65,
LOWE.
Henry of Loudoun Co. 60-62,
LOWRY.
William 99,
LOWRY & CO.
Messrs. 100,
LUCAS.
Robert 40, 41,
LUKE.
John 43,

LYLE.
Robert 46, 109, 110.
Robert deced. 78-82,
Robert an Exr. of Robert deced. 78-82,
Robert Senr. 82,

McINTOSH.
Loy 40, 41,
McCLISH.
Archibald 46,
McLANE
Samuel 109, 110.

MAGRUDER.
Samuel W. Gent., Justice Montgomery Co. Mary
land 106,
MANDEVILLE
John 101,
MARSHALL.
Charles 92, 93, 107,
Thomas 64,
William 107,
MARTIN.
Thomas Bryan, a Surviving Exr. of Thomas Lord
Fairfax 52-54,
MARYLAND.
Annapolis 96, 104,
Charles Co. 51,
Currency of 27, 28, 95, 96, 105, 106,
General Court of the Western Shore 95,
George Town 97, 106,
Montgomery Co. 106,
Prince George Co. 50, 51,
Province of 51,
St. Mary's Co. 27, 28,
MASON.
Abraham Barnes Thompson 71-73,
George of Fairfax Co. 49-51,
Stephen Thompson 72, 73, 89, 91,
MAURY.
Benjamin 6,
MAUZY.
John 80, 82, 109, 111.
MILLS.
John, deced. 92-94,
MINOR.
37,
George, Sub Sheriff, Fairfax Co. 105,
John 107.
J. Junr., Attorney 23, 103, 104,
MINTER.
Edward 109, 111,
MITCHELL.
James 80, 82,
MONROE.
M. 43,
MOORE.
Cleon 19, 77, 78,
Hugh 100, 101,
John of Loudoun Co. 31, 89-91,
MOORE & CRAWFORD
99,

MORRISON.
 John 47,
MOTHERWELL.
 James 47,
MUIR.
 John 41-44,
 John, deced. 44,
MURRAY.
 John & Co. 59, 60,
MUSCHETT.
 James of Pr. William Co. 1-4, 104,
MUSE.
 Battaile of Berkeley Co. 109-111.

NEGROES.
 Dick, suit of 21, 22,
 Sale of to Cleon Moore 77,
NELSON.
 Joseph 34, 35, 54,
NEWTON.
 James 24,

PAGE.
 Mann, Gdn of John Tayloe 95,
PARK.
 James 30,
PATTERSON.
 John 80, 82,
PEACHY.
 William Exr. of Henry Armistead, deced. 22-24,
PENNSYLVANIA
 Currency of 98, 100,
PETTIT.
 Obediah 107,
PHILADELPHIA
 In Prince William Co. 37, 99, 100, 101,
POLLARD.
 Thomas, Gent. Justice Fairfax Co. 2,
POTTS.
 John 56-58,
 John Junr. 77,
 John Junr. Justice Fairfax Co. 43,
POWELL.
 William of Prince William Co., an Admr. of
    Benjamin Edwards, Senr. 6-8,
PRICE.
 Robert 28,
PURCELL.
 George 63,

QUANTICO WAREHOUSE
 109,

RAMSAY.
 Dennis of Alexandria in Fairfax Co. 66-70, 96-98,
    111,
RANDOLPH.
 Edmund, Attorney 3,
RATCLIFFE.
 Shadrack 34, 35, 54,
REED
 William 101,

REEDER.
 Thomas 95, 96.
 Thomas, deced. 96.
RENSHAW.
 Hosea 77,
RIVER.
 Potomack 83, 94,
ROBINSON, SANDESON & CO.
 25, 26,
ROBINSON, SANDERSON & RUMNEY
 Alexandria Merchants 14-16,
RUMNEY.
 John 16,

SANDFORD
 Richard 43,
SCHOLFIELD / SCOLEFIELD
 Thomas of Loudoun Co. 88-92.
SCOTT.
 David Willson 54-56,
 David Willson & Co. 63, 64,
 Richard 109,
 Richard M. 65, 104,
 William 101,
SHOLL.
 Charles 77,
SIMMS.
 Charles, Attorney 8, 9, 10, 13, 18, 20, 22, 27, 31,
    36, 38, 40, 41, 47, 48, 57, 59, 67, 70, 74, 84,
    85, 87, 93, 94, 96, 97, 102-104, 106, 110,
 Charles an Admr. of John Mills, deced. 92-94,
SKINKER.
 William of Pr. William Co. 29, 38, 54-56,
SLAUGHTER,
 Anne, Mrs. 11, 17-19.
SMITH.
 James 109, 111.
 William 47,
SON.
 Francis, otherwise called Francis Jackson 3, 4,
STABLER.
 William of Loudoun Co. 87,
STEPHENS.
 William, Dep. Sheriff Loudoun Co. 21,
STITH.
 Buckner of Fairfax Co. 1, 17, 18, 30,
 Buckner of Fairfax Co., deced. 2, 31,
STODDART.
 Benjamin 96-98,
STUART / STEWART
 David 102, 103,
 Hugh of Pr. William Co. 3, 4, 60-62, 101,
SUITS.
 Alexander & Muschett v Stith & Boggess 1-2.
 Armistead's Exr. v Carter's Admrs. 22-24,
 Armstrong v Jones 26-28,
 Arnold v Arnold 94, 95.
 Bennett v Herbert 47-49.
 Bennett v Herbert 101-103,
 Cawood v Reeder 95, 96.
 Cockran v Grant & Blackwell 4-6,
 Conn v West 36.

Heritage Books by Ruth and Sam Sparacio

Abstracts of Account Books of Edward Dixon,
Merchant of Port Royal, Virginia, Volume I: 1743–1747

Abstracts of Account Books of Edward Dixon,
Merchant of Port Royal, Virginia, Volume II

Albemarle County, Virginia Deed and Will Book Abstracts, 1748–1752

Albemarle County, Virginia Deed Book Abstracts, 1758–1761

Albemarle County, Virginia Deed Book Abstracts, 1761–1764

Albemarle County, Virginia Deed Book Abstracts, 1764–1768

Albemarle County, Virginia Deed Book Abstracts, 1768–1770

Albemarle County, Virginia Deed Book Abstracts, 1771–1772

Albemarle County, Virginia Deed Book Abstracts, 1772–1776

Albemarle County, Virginia Deed Book Abstracts, 1776–1778

Albemarle County, Virginia Deed Book Abstracts, 1778–1780

Albemarle County, Virginia Deed Book Abstracts, 1780–1783

Albemarle County, Virginia Deed Book Abstracts, 1783–1785

Albemarle County, Virginia Deed Book Abstracts, 1785–1787

Albemarle County, Virginia Deed Book Abstracts, 1787–1790

Albemarle County, Virginia Deed Book Abstracts, 1790–1791

Albemarle County, Virginia Deed Book Abstracts, 1791–1793

Albemarle County, Virginia Deed Book Abstracts, 1793–1794

Albemarle County, Virginia Deed Book Abstracts, 1794–1795

Albemarle County, Virginia Deed Book Abstracts, 1795–1796

Albemarle County, Virginia Deed Book Abstracts, 1796–1797

Albemarle County, Virginia Will Book Abstracts:
1752–1756 and 1775–1783

Albemarle County, Virginia Will Book: 2, 1752–1764

Albemarle County, Virginia Wills, 1764–1775

Albemarle County, Virginia Will Book: 3, 1785–1798

Augusta County, Virginia Land Tax Books, 1782–1788

Augusta County, Virginia Land Tax Books, 1788 1790

Amherst County, Virginia Land Tax Books, 1789–1791

Caroline County, Virginia Appeals and Land Causes, 1787–1794

Caroline County, Virginia Appeals and Land Causes, 1795–1800

Caroline County, Virginia Committee of Safety and Early Surveys,
1729–1762 and 1774–1775

Caroline County, Virginia Guardian Bonds 1806–1821

Caroline County, Virginia Land Tax Book Alterations, 1782–1789

Caroline County, Virginia Land Tax Book Alterations, 1789–1792

Caroline County, Virginia Land Tax Book Alterations, 1792–1795

Caroline County, Virginia Land Tax Book Alterations, 1795–1798

Caroline County, Virginia Order Book Abstracts, 1765

Caroline County, Virginia Order Book Abstracts, 1767–1768

Caroline County, Virginia Order Book Abstracts, 1768–1770

Caroline County, Virginia Order Book Abstracts, 1770–1771

Caroline County, Virginia Order Book, 1764

Caroline County, Virginia Order Book, 1765–1767

Caroline County, Virginia Order Book, 1771–1772

Caroline County, Virginia Order Book, 1772–1773

Caroline County, Virginia Order Book, 1773

Caroline County, Virginia Order Book, 1773–1774

Caroline County, Virginia Order Book, 1774–1778

Caroline County, Virginia Order Book, 1778–1781

Caroline County, Virginia Order Book, 1781–1783

Caroline County, Virginia Order Book, 1783–1784

Caroline County, Virginia Order Book, 1784–1785

Caroline County, Virginia Order Book, 1785–1786

Caroline County, Virginia Order Book, 1786–1787

Caroline County, Virginia Order Book, 1787, Part 1

Caroline County, Virginia Order Book, 1787, Part 2

Caroline County, Virginia Order Book, 1787–1788

Caroline County, Virginia Order Book, 1788

Culpeper County, Virginia Deed Book Abstracts, 1769–1773

Culpeper County, Virginia Deed Book Abstracts,1778–1779

Culpeper County, Virginia Deed Book Abstracts, 1781–1783

Culpeper County, Virginia Deed Book Abstracts, 1785–1786

Culpeper County, Virginia Deed Book Abstracts,1788–1789

Culpeper County, Virginia Deed Book Abstracts, 1791–1792

Culpeper County, Virginia Deed Book Abstracts, 1795–1796

Culpeper County, Virginia Land Tax Book, 1782–1786

Culpeper County, Virginia Land Tax Book, 1787–1789

Culpeper County, Virginia Minute Book, 1763–1764

Digest of Family Relationships, 1650–1692,
from Virginia County Court Records

Digest of Family Relationships, 1720–1750,
from Virginia County Court Records

Digest of Family Relationships, 1750–1763,
from Virginia County Court Records

Digest of Family Relationships, 1764–1775,
from Virginia County Court Records

Essex County, Virginia Deed and Will Abstracts, 1695–1697

Essex County, Virginia Deed and Will Abstracts, 1697–1699

Essex County, Virginia Deed and Will Abstracts, 1699–1701

Essex County, Virginia Deed and Will Abstracts, 1701–1703

Essex County, Virginia Deed and Will Book, 1692–1693

Essex County, Virginia Deed and Will Book, 1693–1694

Essex County, Virginia Deed and Will Book, 1694–1695

Essex County, Virginia Deed and Will Book, 1695–1697

Essex County, Virginia Deed and Will Book, 1697–1699

Essex County, Virginia Deed and Will Book, 1701–1704

Essex County, Virginia Deed and Will Book, 1745–1749

Essex County, Virginia Deed, 1753–1754 and Will Book 1750

Essex County, Virginia Deed Abstracts, 1721–1724

Essex County, Virginia Deed Book, 1724–1728

Essex County, Virginia Deed Book, 1728–1733

Essex County, Virginia Deed Book, 1733–1738

Essex County, Virginia Deed Book, 1738–1742

Essex County, Virginia Deed Book, 1742–1745

Essex County, Virginia Deed Abstracts, 1745–1749

Essex County, Virginia Deed Book, 1749–1751

Essex County, Virginia Deed Book, 1751–1753

Essex County, Virginia Land Trials Abstracts, 1711–1741

Essex County, Virginia Order Book Abstracts, 1695–1699

Essex County, Virginia Order Book Abstracts, 1699–1702

Essex County, Virginia Order Book Abstracts, 1716–1723, Part 1

Essex County, Virginia Order Book Abstracts, 1716–1723, Part 2

Essex County, Virginia Order Book Abstracts, 1716–1723, Part 3

Essex County, Virginia Order Book Abstracts, 1716–1723, Part 4

Essex County, Virginia Order Book Abstracts, 1723–1725, Part 1

Essex County, Virginia Order Book Abstracts, 1723–1725, Part 2

Essex County, Virginia Order Book Abstracts, 1725–1729, Part 1

Essex County, Virginia Order Book Abstracts, 1727–1729, Part 2

Essex County, Virginia Order Book, 1695–1699

Essex County, Virginia Will Abstracts, 1730–1735

Essex County, Virginia Will Abstracts, 1735–1743

Loudoun County, Virginia Deed Book Abstracts, 1774–1775
Loudoun County, Virginia Deed Book Abstracts, 1775–1778
Loudoun County, Virginia Deed Book Abstracts, 1778–1779
Loudoun County, Virginia Deed Book Abstracts, 1779–1782
Loudoun County, Virginia Deed Book Abstracts, 1782–1784
Loudoun County, Virginia Deed Book Abstracts, 1784–1785
Loudoun County, Virginia Deed Book Abstracts, 1785–1786
Loudoun County, Virginia Deed Book Abstracts, 1787–1788
Loudoun County, Virginia Deed Book Abstracts, 1789–1790
Loudoun County, Virginia Deed Book Abstracts, 1790–1792
Loudoun County, Virginia Deed Book Abstracts, 1793–1794
Loudoun County, Virginia Deed Book Abstracts, 1794–1795
Loudoun County, Virginia Deed Book Abstracts, 1795–1796
Loudoun County, Virginia Deed Book Abstracts, 1796
Loudoun County, Virginia Order Book Abstracts, 1757–1758
Loudoun County, Virginia Order Book Abstracts, 1758–1759
Loudoun County, Virginia Order Book Abstracts, 1761–1762
Loudoun County, Virginia Order Book Abstracts, 1762
Loudoun County, Virginia Order Book Abstracts, 1762–1763
Loudoun County, Virginia Order Book Abstracts, 1763–1764
Loudoun County, Virginia Order Book Abstracts, 1764
Loudoun County, Virginia Titheable Lists, 1758–1769
Loudoun County, Virginia Will Book Abstracts, 1757–1771
Loudoun County, Virginia Will Book Abstracts, 1772–1782
Loudoun County, Virginia Will Book Abstracts, 1783–1788
Louisa County, Virginia Deed Book Abstracts, 1742–1744
Louisa County, Virginia Deed Book Abstracts, 1744–1746
Louisa County, Virginia Order Book, 1742–1744
Louisa County, Virginia, Orders, 1744–1747
Louisa County, Virginia Orders 1747–1748, 1766, and 1772
Louisa County, Virginia, Orders, 1772–1774
Louisa County, Virginia, Order Book Abstracts, 1767–1768
Louisa County, Virginia, Orders, 1769–1770
Louisa County, Virginia, Orders, 1770–1772
Louisa County, Virginia, Orders, 1772–1774
Madison County, Virginia Deed Book Abstracts, 1793–1804
Madison County, Virginia Deed Book, 1793–1813,
and Marriage Bonds, 1793–1800

Middlesex County, Virginia Deed Book Abstracts, 1679–1688
Middlesex County, Virginia Deed Book Abstracts, 1688–1694
Middlesex County, Virginia Deed Book Abstracts, 1694–1703
Middlesex County, Virginia Deed Book Abstracts, 1703–1709
Middlesex County, Virginia Deed Book Abstracts, 1709–1720
Middlesex County, Virginia Order Book Abstracts, 1680–1686
Middlesex County, Virginia Order Book Abstracts, 1686–1690
Middlesex County, Virginia Order Book Abstracts, 1694–1697
Middlesex County, Virginia Order Book Abstracts, 1697–1700
Middlesex County, Virginia Order Book Abstracts, 1700–1702
Middlesex County, Virginia Order Book Abstracts, 1705–1707
Middlesex County, Virginia Order Book Abstracts, 1707–1708
Middlesex County, Virginia Order Book Abstracts, 1708–1710
Middlesex County, Virginia Order Book Abstracts, 1710–1712
Middlesex County, Virginia Order Book Abstracts, 1712–1714
Middlesex County, Virginia Order Book Abstracts, 1714–1716
Middlesex County, Virginia Order Book Abstracts, 1716–1719
Middlesex County, Virginia Order Book Abstracts, 1719–1721
Middlesex County, Virginia Order Book Abstracts, 1721–1724

Middlesex County, Virginia Order Book Abstracts, 1732–1737
Middlesex County, Virginia Order Book Abstracts, 1740–1745
Middlesex County, Virginia Record Book Abstracts, 1721–1813
Northumberland County, Virginia Deed and Will Book, 1650–1655
Northumberland County, Virginia Deed and Will Book, 1655–1658
Northumberland County, Virginia Deed and Will Book, 1658–1662
Northumberland County, Virginia Deed and Will Book, 1662–1666
Northumberland County, Virginia Deed and Will Book, 1666–1670
Northumberland County, Virginia Deed and Will Book,
1670–1672 and 1706–1711
Northumberland County, Virginia Deed and Will Book, 1711–1712
Northumberland County, Virginia Deed and Will Book, 1712–1726
Northumberland County, Virginia Order Book, 1652–1657
Northumberland County, Virginia Order Book, 1657–1661
Northumberland County, Virginia Order Book, 1661–1665
Northumberland County, Virginia Order Book, 1665–1669
Northumberland County, Virginia Order Book, 1669–1673
Northumberland County, Virginia Order Book, 1674–1677
Northumberland County, Virginia Order Book, 1677–1679
Northumberland County, Virginia Order Book, 1680–1683
Northumberland County, Virginia Order Book, 1683–1686
Northumberland County, Virginia Order Book, 1699–1700
Northumberland County, Virginia Order Book, 1700–1702
Northumberland County, Virginia Order Book, 1702–1704
Orange County, Virginia, Chancery Suits, 1831–1845
Orange County, Virginia Deeds, 1743–1759
Orange County, Virginia Deed Book Abstracts, 1759–1778
Orange County, Virginia Deed Book Abstracts, 1778–1786
Orange County, Virginia Deed Book Abstracts, 1795–1797
Orange County, Virginia Deed Book Abstracts, 1797–1799
Orange County, Virginia Deed Book Abstracts, 1799–1800
Orange County, Virginia Deed Book Abstracts, 1800–1802
Orange County, Virginia Deed Book Abstracts, 1786–1791, Deed Book 19
Orange County, Virginia Deed Book Abstracts, 1791–1795, Deed Book 20
Orange County, Virginia Deed Book Abstracts, 1795–1797, Deed Book 21
Orange County, Virginia, Digest of Will Abstracts, 1734–1838
Orange County, Virginia Land Tax Book, 1782–1790
Orange County, Virginia Land Tax Book, 1791–1795
Orange County, Virginia Order Book Abstracts, 1747–1748
Orange County, Virginia Order Book Abstracts, 1748–1749
Orange County, Virginia Order Book Abstracts, 1749–1752
Orange County, Virginia Order Book Abstracts, 1752–1753
Orange County, Virginia Order Book Abstracts, 1753–1754
Orange County, Virginia Order Book Abstracts, 1755–1756
Orange County, Virginia Order Book Abstracts, 1756–1757
Orange County, Virginia Order Book Abstracts, 1757–1759
Orange County, Virginia Order Book Abstracts, 1759–1762
Orange County, Virginia Order Book Abstracts, 1762–1763
Orange County, Virginia Will Abstracts, 1778–1821
Orange County, Virginia Will Abstracts, 1821–1838
Orange County, Virginia, Will Digest, 1734–1838
Pamunkey Neighbors of Orange County, Virginia (Transcriptions from the original files of County Courts in Virginia, Kentucky and Missouri of wills, deeds, order books & marriages as well as some family lines...)
A Supplement to Pamunkey Neighbors of Orange County, Virginia, Volumes 1 and 2
Ruth and Sam Sparacio, Luretta and Eldon Corkill

Stafford County, Virginia Order Book, 1664–1668 and 1689–1690

Stafford County, Virginia Order Book, 1691–1692

Stafford County, Virginia Order Book, 1692–1693

Stafford County, Virginia Will Book, 1729–1748

Stafford County, Virginia Will Book, 1748–1767

Westmoreland County, Virginia Deed and Will Abstracts, 1723–1726

Westmoreland County, Virginia Deed and Will Abstracts, 1726–1729

Westmoreland County, Virginia Deed and Will Abstracts, 1729–1732

Westmoreland County, Virginia Deed and Will Abstracts, 1732–1734

Westmoreland County, Virginia Deed and Will Abstracts, 1734–1736

Westmoreland County, Virginia Deed and Will Abstracts, 1736–1740

Westmoreland County, Virginia Deed and Will Abstracts, 1740–1742

Westmoreland County, Virginia Deed and Will Abstracts, 1742–1745

Westmoreland County, Virginia Deed and Will Abstracts, 1745–1747

Westmoreland County, Virginia Deed and Will Abstracts, 1747–1748

Westmoreland County, Virginia Deed and Will Abstracts, 1749–1751

Westmoreland County, Virginia Deed and Will Abstracts, 1751–1754

Westmoreland County, Virginia Deed and Will Abstracts, 1754–1756

Westmoreland County, Virginia Order Book, 1705–1707

Westmoreland County, Virginia Order Book, 1707–1709

Westmoreland County, Virginia Order Book, 1709–1712

Westmoreland County, Virginia Order Book, 1712–1714

Westmoreland County, Virginia Order Book, 1714–1716

Westmoreland County, Virginia Order Book, 1716–1718

Westmoreland County, Virginia Order Book, 1718–1721

www.ingramcontent.com/pod-product-compliance
Lightning Source LLC
Chambersburg PA
CBHW080336270326
41927CB00014B/3244